U0098215

序　言

　　學了多年的英文，在面對老外的時候，您是否仍有「一言難盡」的遺憾呢？

　　為了幫助讀者加強口語能力，學習出版社與欣語社合作，推出「*You Can Call Me*」一書。您只需要打通電話，配合本書的內容，就可以和「克拉瑪空中外語交談園地」的外籍老師練習英語對話。這種方便、新穎、經濟的學習外語方式，讓您在家就可說英語，免除出門塞車之苦，達到事半功倍的效果。

　　本書收錄各式各樣的交談話題，從休閒的電影、音樂、旅遊，以及敏感的政治話題，甚至尖端科技的網際網路 (Internet) 都有涉獵。豐富的題材與生動的會話內容，讓您拿起話筒，便能與外籍老師侃侃而談，在增強會話能力之餘，也拓展您的生活視野。本書並附錄各類實用語彙與珍貴資料，豐富您的英文知識，加倍學習的效果。

　　本書在編校過程中雖力求完善，然疏漏之處恐所難免，誠盼各界先進不吝指正。

編者　謹識

CONTENTS

只要拿起電話撥(02)751-6278，您
就可以練習英語會話。詳細內容請
參閱本書 202 頁。

1. Self-Introduction 自我介紹

📞 *打電話問老師問題*

1. How long have you been in Taiwan？你來台灣多久了？

2. Where are you from？你來自那裡？

3. Are you here on business？你是來這兒工作嗎？

4. What kind of work do you do？你從事何種工作？

5. Do you speak Chinese？你會說中文嗎？

6. Have you ever studied Chinese？你學過中文嗎？

7. Are you a student？你是學生嗎？

8. What do you think about Taiwan？
你對台灣有何看法？

9. Are you familiar with the culture here in Taiwan？
你熟悉台灣的文化嗎？

10. What part of the culture do you like best？
你最喜歡那一方面的文化？

11. How long do you plan to spend in Taiwan？
你計畫在台灣待多久？

12. What in Taiwan do you like best？
台灣有什麼是你最喜歡的？

☎ *打電話和老師討論問題*

Dialogue 1

老師 : My name is Henry. What's your name ?
我的名字是亨利。你叫什麼名字？

學生 : I am Sharon. How are your doing ?
我是雪倫。你好嗎？

老師 : Just fine. Is this the first time you have called ?
很好。這是你第一次打電話來嗎？

學生 : Yes. My friend is a member of your language club, and he encouraged me to call you if I want to improve my spoken English.
是的。我朋友是你們語言社的會員，他鼓勵我若想增進英文口語的能力，可以打電話給你們。

老師 : Are you a student ?
你是學生嗎？

學生 : Now I am a *part-time student*. I have to work part-time to pay my tuition. I also study at a cram school, so I can *get a better score on* the English language exams I have to take to study abroad.
我現在是個工讀生。我必須花部分時間工作，支付我的學費。我也在一所補習班上課，以便能在留學英文考試中，得到較好的成績。
➜ tuition (tjuˈɪʃən) *n.* 學費   *cram school* 補習班

老師 : Do you know any foreigners ?
你有認識的外國人嗎？

學生 : When I was studying English at language school, I met quite a few of them, mostly Americans.
我在語言學校學英文時，有碰到很多，大部分是美國人。

Dialogue 2

老師：Have you lived in Taiwan all your life?
你一直住在台灣嗎？

學生：Yes, I was born in Taipei in 1972. My parents were born here, too. My family has been in Taiwan for many generations.
是的，我於 1972 年生於台北。我的父母也是在這兒出生，我的家族在台灣已經有好幾代了。

老師：Would you say that you are a typical Taiwanese?
你覺得你是個典型的台灣人嗎？

學生：I think so. My parents are fairly open, but nevertheless my family still *regards tradition with respect*. There are some things which are just basic principles and deserve to be respected.
我想是的。我的父母相當開明，但是我們家仍然尊重傳統。有些事情是很基本的原則，值得去尊重。

老師：Given the choice, would you choose to have been born in Taiwan or another country?
若讓你選擇，你會選擇出生在台灣，或是其他的國家？

學生：I've never lived in another country for a long period of time, but considering the news I hear from the media and my friends and relatives abroad, I would say that I prefer Taiwan. It has many problems, but I still like it.
我從沒有在其他國家長時間居住過，但是從媒體，以及我在國外的親戚朋友那兒得到的消息，我會說我寧願選擇台灣。雖然有許多的問題，但我還是喜歡這裡。

** ———————————

generation (ˌdʒɛnəˈreʃən) *n.* 世代　　typical (ˈtɪpɪkl̩) *adj.* 典型的
nevertheless (ˌnɛvəðəˈlɛs) *adv.* 然而　　principle (ˈprɪnsəpl̩) *n.* 原則
media (ˈmidɪə) *n. pl.* 媒體（單數形為 medium (ˈmidɪəm)）

Dialogue 3

老師： Do you like Chinese culture ?
你喜歡中國文化嗎？

學生： It's not a matter of liking it or not. I don't like it or
dislike it. I think some of the traditions are very good,
and some are *out of date*. Regardless of what we think
about Chinese culture, I feel everyone should respect it.
這不是喜不喜歡的問題，我不喜歡也不討厭它。我想有一些傳統是
很好，有一些則過時了。然而，不管我們怎麼想，我覺得我們都應
該尊重它。

老師： Do you think that the growing Western influence on
Taiwan will change the face of Chinese culture ?
你認為，與日俱增的西方文化對台灣的影響，會改變中國文化的面
貌嗎？

學生： I think it already has. Western culture has *infiltrated
Taiwan via the media*, and a lot of young people are
becoming more like Westerners. I think it is a good
thing to experience other cultures, but we have to preserve our own, too !
我想已經有所改變。西方文化已藉由大眾媒體滲入台灣，許多年輕
人變得像西方人。我覺得能夠體驗其他文化是件好事，但是我們也
必須保存自己的！

** ───────────────────
out of date 過時的   regardless (rɪ'gɑrdlɪs) *adj.* 不顧
influence ('ɪnfluəns) *n.* 影響   infiltrate (ɪn'fɪltret) *v.* 滲透
via ('vaɪə) *prep.* 經由   Westerner ('wɛstənə) *n.* 西方人
preserve (prɪ'zɝv) *v.* 保護；保存

老師：Are you happy with what you have in life so far?
你對目前生活中所擁有的感到快樂嗎？

學生：Parents always tell their kids how fortunate they are to have been born in this day and age. I used to discard it, but now that I'm older it's making sense.
父母親總是告訴孩子，他們能生在今天這個時代是多麼幸運。我以前都不理會這種想法，可是現在年紀大了，這句話變得有意義了。

I mean, if I had been born in another country, I might not have had the opportunities, rights and privileges that I *take for granted* now.
我的意思是說，如果我生在其他國家，我現在就沒有這些我視為理所當然的機會、權利及特權。

**

---

discard〔dɪs'kɑrd〕v. 拋棄；放棄　　*make sense* 有意義
take for granted 認為理所當然　　opportunity〔͵ɑpə'tjunətɪ〕n. 機會
privilege〔'prɪvəlɪdʒ〕n. 特權

> ### 溝通技巧

和外國老師談話時，可以利用以下的問題來幫助溝通：

- ◆ How do you spell that word? 那個字要怎麼拼？
- ◆ What does that word mean? 那個字是什麼意思？
- ◆ Excuse me, could you repeat that? 對不起，你能再重覆一次嗎？
- ◆ Is there a better way to say that? 有沒有較好的說法呢？
- ◆ What is the difference between A and B? A和B有什麼不同呢？
- ◆ Can you give me an example? 你能舉個例子嗎？
- ◆ Can you correct my grammar as we speak?
  在我們講話時，你能糾正我的文法嗎？

2. *Movies* 電 影

📞 *打電話問老師問題*

1. What kind of movies do you like ? 你喜歡那一類型的電影 ?

2. What is your favorite movie? 你最喜歡那部電影 ?

3. Do you like to watch movies at the theater or at the MTV ? 你喜歡到戲院或是 MTV 看電影 ?

4. Who is your favorite actor ? 你最喜歡的男演員是誰 ?

5. Who is your favorite actress ? 你最喜歡的女演員是誰 ?

6. What was the best movie you ever saw ?
   你看過最棒的電影是什麼 ?

7. Why did you like it ? 你為什麼喜歡它 ?

8. What was the worst movie you ever saw ?
   你看過最爛的電影是什麼 ?

9. Why didn't you like it ? 你為什麼不喜歡它 ?

10. How often do you go to the movies ?
    你多久看一次電影 ?

11. Have you seen any good movies lately ?
    你最近看過什麼好電影 ?

12. Do you like VCR movies ? 你喜歡看錄影帶嗎 ?

打電話和老師討論問題

Dialogue 1

老師： What kind of movies do you like ?
你喜歡那一類型的電影？

學生： I like to watch adventure movies because they take me into another world, one which is interesting and far more exciting than in the real world.
我喜歡看冒險片，因爲它引領我進入另一個世界，比現實生活來得有趣且更刺激。

老師： What is your favorite movie ?
你最喜歡那部電影？

學生： My favorite movie is "Pulp Fiction." It has an exciting plot, has an excellent cast and the direction and production is simply superb.
我最喜歡的電影是「黑色追緝令」。它的劇情精彩、卡司強大、導演和製作都極爲出色。

老師： Do you like to watch movies at the theater or at the MTV ?
你喜歡到戲院或是 MTV 看電影？

學生： I like to watch movies at the theater.
我喜歡到戲院看電影。

** ─────────────

adventure (əd'vɛntʃə) n. 冒險　　pulp (pʌlp) n. 廉價低級之物
fiction ('fɪkʃən) n. 小說　　plot (plat) n. 情節
cast (kæst) n. 演員的陣容　　superb (su'pɝb) adj. 出色的
MTV = *Movie Television*

老師： Oh, really？ I thought people in Taiwan liked to watch movies at the MTV because MTV houses are everywhere.

真的嗎？我以為台灣的人喜歡到 MTV 看電影，因為你們的 MTV 到處林立。

學生： I think most people like to watch movies at the theater. The picture is better because of the bigger screen, and you can sense if the movie is good or bad by the reaction of the audience. If it's a good movie, you will be *surrounded by applause and laughter*!

我想大部分的人喜歡到戲院看電影。它的螢幕大，影像較好，而且你可以從觀眾的反應，知道片子好不好。如果是部好片，你會置身鼓掌與笑聲之中。

Dialogue 2

老師： Who is your favorite actress？
你最喜歡的女演員是誰？

學生： My favorite actress is Jane Fonda. In all the movies she has appeared in, she comes across as being very confident as well as intelligent, and I also enjoy her witty remarks.

我最喜歡的女演員是珍・芳達。在她演出的電影中，她給人自信又聰明的印象，我也欣賞她機智的言談。

I think "9 to 5" was her best movie because the role she played was a good *example for modern women*.

我認為「九點到五點」是她最棒的電影，因為她所飾演的角色，是現代女性的模範。

**

audience (ˈɔdɪəns) *n.* 觀眾　　surround (səˈraʊnd) *v.* 包圍
applause (əˈplɔz) *n.* 鼓掌　　*come across as* 給人～印象
confident (ˈkɑnfədənt) *adj.* 自信的　　intelligent (ɪnˈtɛlədʒənt) *adj.* 聰明的
witty (ˈwɪtɪ) *adj.* 機智的　　remark (rɪˈmɑrk) *n.* 言論

老師：Who is your favorite actor?
　　　你最喜歡的男演員是誰？

學生：My favorite actor is Paul Newman. I have seen most
　　　of his movies. In every movie his portrayal of the role
　　　is always precise. He knows what he wants, and does
　　　what he has to do, so I think he is a good actor.
　　　我最喜歡的男演員是保羅·紐曼，我幾乎看遍他所有的電影。在每
　　　齣戲中，他對角色的詮釋一向很精準，他知道自己想要什麼，並且
　　　克盡職責，所以我認爲他是個好演員。

Dialogue 3

老師：What was the best movie you ever saw?
　　　你看過最棒的電影是什麼？

學生：The best movie I ever saw was "The Professional."
　　　我看過最好的電影是「終極追殺令」。

老師：Why did you like it?
　　　你爲什麼喜歡它？

學生：I liked it because it really made me think. It had a
　　　superb combination of screenplay, direction and exe-
　　　cution backed up by an excellent line of actors and
　　　actresses. It was able to *capture the imagination of*
　　　the audience.
　　　我喜歡它，因爲它眞的引發我思考。這部片的劇本、導演、手法都
　　　很出色，演員陣容也極堅強。它能夠吸引觀衆的想像力。

**
portrayal〔por'treəl〕*n.* 扮演　　screenplay〔'skrin‚ple〕*n.* 劇本
back〔bæk〕*v.* 支持　　capture〔'kæptʃə〕*v.* 捕捉
imagination〔‚ɪmædʒə'neʃən〕*n.* 想像力

老師： What was the worst movie you ever saw ?
你看過最爛的電影是什麼？

學生： "Oscar." I didn't like it because everything was disastrous from the very beginning.
「彈指威龍」。我不喜歡它，因為從片子一開始就是一團糟。

The movie itself had a large budget but it was wasted. The story was lousy, full of clichés and predictable. In addition, Sylvester Stallone was not suitable for the leading role.
電影本身的預算龐大且浪費，故事無聊、流於陳腔濫調，而且都可預知。此外，主角由席維斯・史特龍來飾演也不適合。

**

disastrous (dɪ'zæstrəs) *adj.* 災難的   budget ('bʌdʒɪt) *n.* 預算
lousy ('laʊzɪ) *adj.* 無聊的   cliché (klɪ'ʃe) *n.* 陳腔濫調
predictable (prɪ'dɪktəb̩l) *adj.* 可預測的

電影類別

action film 動作片	kung fu film 武俠片
comedy film 喜劇片	science film 科幻片
romance film 文藝片	cartoons 卡通片
musical film 音樂片	Western film 西部片
drama film 劇情片	documentary (,dɑkjə'mɛntərɪ) 紀錄片
horror film 恐怖片	Disney (Family) 迪士尼家庭電影

賣座名片

Gone with the Wind 亂世佳人
My Fair Lady 窈窕淑女
Roman Holiday 羅馬假期
The Sound of Music 眞善美
Love Story 愛的故事
Casablanca 北非諜影
Rear Window 後窗
The Exorcist 大法師
Dressed to Kill 剃刀邊緣
Ordinary People 凡夫俗子
Tootsie 窈窕淑男
The Omen 天魔
Godfather 教父
Superman 超人
Rocky ('rɑkɪ) 洛基
Rambo ('ræmbo) 第一滴血
Out of Africa 遠離非洲
Top Gun 悍衛戰士
Rainman 雨人
Beverly Hills Cop
　比佛利山超級警探
Aliens 異形

Fatal Attraction 致命的吸引力
Die Hard 終極警探
Total Recall 魔鬼總動員
Terminator 魔鬼終結者
Lethal Weapon 致命武器
Ghost 第六感生死戀
Indecent Proposal 桃色交易
Basic Instinct 第六感追緝令
The Little Mermaid 小美人魚
The Lion King 獅子王
The Firm 黑色豪門企業
Jurassic Park 侏羅紀公園
The Fugitive 絕命追殺令
Under Siege 魔鬼戰將
Speed 捍衛戰警
True Lies 魔鬼大帝
Forrest Gump 阿甘正傳
Home Alone 小鬼當家
Free Willy 威鯨闖天關
The Mask 摩登大聖
Four Weddings and a Funeral
　你是我今生的新娘

Casablanca (ˌkɑsə'blɑŋkə ,ˌkæsə'blæŋkə) n. 卡薩布蘭加 (摩洛哥城市)
exorcist ('ɛksɔrˌsɪst) n. 驅邪之人；法師　　tootsie ('tutsi) adj. 親愛的
omen ('omən ,'omɪn) n. 預兆　　alien ('elɪən ,'eljən) n. 外星人
fatal ('fetl) adj. 致命的　　recall (rɪ'kɔl) n. 想起
terminator ('tɝməˌnetə) n. 終結者　　lethal ('liθəl) adj. 致命的
indecent (ɪn'disnt) adj. 猥褻的；下流的
instinct ('ɪnstɪŋkt) n. 本能；直覺　　mermaid ('mɝˌmed) n. 美人魚
fugitive ('fjudʒətɪv) n. 逃亡者　　siege (sidʒ) n. 包圍攻擊

3. *Music* 音 樂

📞 *打電話問老師問題*

1. What kinds of music do you listen to？你聽那種音樂？

2. On what occasions do you listen to music？
   你什麼時候聽音樂？

3. Do you have a particularly favorite band？
   你有沒有特別喜愛的樂團？

4. Do you think a lot of kids are affected by the music they listen to？
   你是否覺得，很多小孩都受到他們所聽的音樂的影響？

5. How much music do you listen to each day？
   你每天聽多少音樂？

6. What period of music do you think is the best？
   你覺得那個時期的音樂最好？

7. Why do you prefer this type of music？
   你為什麼比較喜歡這類型的音樂？

8. Do you play any instruments at all？你會彈奏任何樂器嗎？

9. How does music affect our culture？音樂如何影響我們的文化？

10. In what ways do you think music unites people？
    你覺得音樂以什麼方式結合人群？

11. In what ways do you think music separates people？
    你覺得音樂以什麼方式區隔人群？

📞 *打電話和老師討論問題*

Dialogue 1

老師： What kinds of music do you listen to?
你聽那種音樂？

學生： I listen to most kinds of music, anything from rap to pop music. If it sounds nice, I buy it.
大部分種類的音樂我都聽，從繞舌歌曲到流行音樂都有。如果音樂聽起來不錯的話，我就會買。

老師： On what occasions do you listen to music?
你什麼時候聽音樂？

學生： It *depends on* the situation. When I am studying, I listen to classical music; when I am trying to relax, I listen to pop music; it really depends on my mood at that time.
看情況。讀書時，我聽古典音樂；當我想放鬆心情時，我聽流行音樂。真的要看當時的心境。

老師： I see. Do you have a particularly favorite band?
我知道了。你有沒有特別喜愛的樂團呢？

學生： I like most of the bands I listen to, but a few favorites are: the Doors, Pink Floyd and Dire Straits.
大部分我聽的樂團我都喜歡，但是一些最喜歡的是：門、平克佛洛依德，以及悲慘窮困。

** ────────────

rap music 繞舌歌曲　*pop music* 流行音樂
occasion〔əˈkeʒən〕*n.* 場合　*depend on* 視~而定
dire〔daɪr〕*adj.* 緊急的　straits〔strets〕*n. pl.* 窮困
Dire Straits 的意思為「悲慘窮困」，但市面上販售的卡帶、CD 誤譯為險峻海峽。

Dialogue 2

老師： Do you think a lot of kids are affected by the music they listen to ?

你是否覺得，很多小孩都受到他們所聽的音樂的影響？

學生： Definitely. Music is an art form, and good music can *reach the hearts* of those who listen to it. That is why it is important to choose the right kind of music.

這是一定的。音樂是種藝術，而且好的音樂能深達聆聽者的心靈。那就是為什麼選擇正確的音樂種類很重要。

老師： How much music do you listen to each day ?

你每天聽多少音樂？

學生： I listen to a lot of music. I always have some music in the background so that I don't feel bored. It helps me think better. I would say that I listen to about 5 hours of music a day.

我聽許多音樂。我總是讓一些音樂當背景，這樣我才不會覺得無聊，那可幫助我思考。可以說我一天聽五小時的音樂。

老師： That is a lot of listening. You must place a lot of emphasis on your music !

那算是聽得很多。你一定很重視你的音樂。

學生： Yes, in fact the first thing I bought when I got some money from my part-time work was a mini hi-fi system. It took me 2 months of work in the summer to earn enough money to buy it.

是啊，事實上當我領到打工賺的錢時，我所買的第一件東西就是小型高傳真音響。它花了我暑假兩個月工作，才賺到足夠的錢來買。

**

place emphasis on 重視；強調　　part-time (ˈpɑrtˈtaɪm) *adj.* 打工的
hi-fi (ˈhaɪˈfaɪ) *n. adj.* 高度傳真 (= high-fidelity)

Dialogue 3

老師： What period of music do you think is the best?
你覺得那個時期的音樂最好？

學生： Each decade has its own special characteristics: In the 50's there was Elvis, in the 60's there was the Beatles, and in the 90's there is now the grunge movement. My favorite era is the disco music of the mid-seventies!
每個時期都有自己獨特的特徵：五〇年代有貓王、六〇年代有披頭四、九〇年代有現在的頹廢搖滾運動。我最喜歡的年代是七〇年代中期的狄斯可音樂。

老師： Why do you prefer this type of music?
你為什麼比較喜歡這類型的音樂？

學生： I grew up in the eighties, and all the sounds of the late-seventies *remind me of* my childhood.
我在八〇年代長大，所有七〇年代晚期的音樂都使我回想起童年。

老師： Do you play any instruments at all?
你會彈奏任何樂器嗎？

學生： I played the trumpet when I was little, but now I am not playing anything. However, I am thinking about *taking up* playing the guitar.
我小時候吹過喇叭，但我現在沒玩任何樂器。不過，我在考慮要開始彈吉他。

**

decade〔ˋdɛked, dɛkˋed〕*n.* 十年   characteristic〔͵kærɪktəˋrɪstɪk〕*n.* 特徵
grunge〔grʌndʒ〕*n.* 垃圾；髒污之物（俚）   era〔ˋɪrə, ˋirə〕*n.* 年代；時代
instrument〔ˋɪnstrəmənt〕*n.* 樂器
trumpet〔ˋtrʌmpɪt〕*n.* 喇叭   *take up* 開始

音樂類別

classical music 古典樂
opera（'ɑpərə）歌劇
jazz（dʒæz）爵士
Dixieland（'dɪksɪˌlænd）
　狄西蘭爵士樂（美國南部音樂）
boogie woogie（'bʊgɪ'wʊgɪ）
　布奇爵士樂
big band 大樂團
jazz fusion 爵士融合樂
fusion（'fjuʒən）*n.* 融合
blues 藍調
soul 靈魂樂
swing music 搖擺樂

pop music 流行音樂
rock n' roll 搖滾樂
heavy metal 重金屬搖滾
acid rock 迷幻搖滾
folk rock 民謠搖滾
punk rock 龐克搖滾
rap（ræp）饒舌樂
country music 鄉村音樂
new age music 新世紀音樂
reggae 雷鬼
folk songs 民歌
disco 狄斯可

樂器種類

trombone（'trɑmbon , tram'bon）伸縮喇叭
euphonium（ju'fonɪəm）低音喇叭
tuba（'tjubə ,'tubə）低音大喇叭
flute（flut）長笛
French horn 法國號
saxophone（'sæksəˌfon）薩克斯風
viola（vɪ'olə ,'vaɪələ）中提琴
double bass 低音提琴
xylophone（'zaɪləˌfon ,'zɪlə-）木琴
organ（'ɔrgən）風琴
piano（pɪ'æno）鋼琴
bass（bæs）貝斯
drum（drʌm）鼓

clarinet（ˌklærə'nɛt）豎笛
harmonica（hɑr'mɑnɪkə）口琴
violin（ˌvaɪə'lɪn）小提琴
cello（'tʃɛlo）大提琴
harp（hɑrp）豎琴
keyboard（'kiˌbord）鍵盤
oboe（'obo）雙簧管
glockenspiel（'glɑkənˌspil）鐵琴
accordion（ə'kɔrdɪən）手風琴
guitar（gɪ'tɑr）吉他

名音樂家

Bach〔bɑk〕巴哈（德國作曲家）

Beethoven〔'betovən〕貝多芬（德國作曲家，樂聖）

Berlioz〔'bɛrlɪˌoz〕白遼士（法國作曲家）

Bizet〔bi'zɛ〕比才（法國作曲家）

Brahms〔brɑmz〕布拉姆斯（德國作曲家、鋼琴家）

Chopin〔'ʃopæn,ʃo'pæn〕蕭邦（波蘭鋼琴家，鋼琴詩人）

Debussy〔də'bjusɪ〕德布西（法國作曲家）

Dvorak〔'dvɔrʒɑk〕德弗札克（捷克作曲家）

Haydn〔'haɪdn̩〕海頓（奧國作曲家）

Johann Strauss〔straʊs〕約翰史特勞斯（奧國作曲家）

Liszt〔lɪst〕李斯特（匈牙利鋼琴家）

Mendelssohn〔'mɛndl̩sn̩〕孟德爾頌（德國作曲家、鋼琴家）

Mozart〔'motsɑrt〕莫札特（奧國作曲家，音樂神童）

Paganini〔ˌpægə'ninɪ〕帕格尼尼（義大利小提琴家）

* * * * *

Puccini〔pu'tʃinɪ〕普契尼（義大利作曲家）

Ravel〔'rævl̩〕拉威爾（法國作曲家）

Rossini〔rɔ'sinɪ〕羅西尼（義大利作曲家）

Rubinstein〔'rubɪnstaɪn〕魯賓斯坦（俄國作曲家、鋼琴家）

Scarlatti〔skɑr'lɑtɪ〕史卡拉第（義大利作曲家，近代歌劇之父）

Schubert〔'ʃubət〕舒伯特（奧國作曲家，歌曲之王）

Schuman〔'ʃumən〕舒曼（德國作曲家）

Shostakovich〔ˌʃɑstə'kovɪtʃ〕蕭士塔高維契（俄國作曲家）

Stravinsky〔strə'vɪnskɪ〕史特拉汶斯基（俄國作曲家）

Tchaikovsky〔tʃaɪ'kɔfskɪ〕柴可夫斯基（俄國作曲家）

Verdi〔'verdɪ〕威爾第（義大利作曲家）

Vivaldi〔vɪ'vɑldɪ〕韋瓦第（義大利作曲家）

Wagner〔'vɑgnə,'wægnə〕華格納（德國作曲家）

Weber〔'wɛbə〕韋伯（德國作曲家）

流行藝人

Ace of Base〔'es əv 'bes〕王牌合唱團
Aerosmith〔'ɛro,smɪθ〕史密斯飛船
Air Supply〔'ɛr sə'plaɪ〕空中補給合唱團
All-4-One 合而為一合唱團
Bee Gees〔'bi 'giz〕比吉斯合唱團
The Beatles 披頭四
Blondie〔'blandi〕金髮美人合唱團
Bon Jovi〔'ban 'dʒovɪ〕邦喬飛合唱團
Chicago〔ʃə'kago〕芝加哥合唱團
Cranberries〔'kræn,bɛrɪz〕小紅莓合唱團
The Eagles 老鷹合唱團
Enigma〔ɪ'nɪgmə〕謎合唱團
Fleetwood Mac〔'flitwud 'mæk〕佛利伍麥克合唱團
New Order 新秩序合唱團
Nirvana〔nɜ'vænə〕超脫合唱團
Queen 皇后合唱團
Rolling Stone 滾石合唱團
Roxette〔rak'sɛt〕羅克塞合唱團
Simply Red 就是紅合唱團
Van Halen〔væn 'hælən〕范海倫合唱團

☆ ☆ ☆ ☆ ☆ ☆ ☆ ☆

Annie Lennox〔'ænɪ 'lɛnɪks〕安妮藍妮克絲
Barbara Streisand〔'barbərə 'straɪsənd〕芭芭拉史翠珊
Bonnie Raitt〔'banɪ 'ræt〕邦妮瑞特
Basia〔'baʃə〕貝莎
Kate Bush〔'kæt 'buʃ〕凱特布希
Carole King〔'kærəl 'kɪŋ〕卡洛金
Cher〔ʃɛr〕雪兒
Diana Rose〔daɪ'ænə 'roz〕黛安娜蘿絲

Debbie Gibson（ˈdɛbɪ ˈgɪbsn̩）黛比吉布森
Enya（ˈɛnjə）恩雅
Gloria Estefan（ˈglorɪə ˈɛstəfən）葛蘿莉亞伊斯特芳
Janet Jackson（ˈdʒænɪt ˈdʒæksn̩）珍娜傑克森
Joan Baez（ˈdʒon ˈbaɪə）瓊拜亞
Madonna（məˈdɑnə）瑪丹娜
Mariah Carey（məˈraɪə ˈkerɪ）瑪麗亞凱莉
Sade（ʃəˈde）夏黛
Sheryl Crow（ˈʃɛrl̩ ˈkro）雪瑞兒可洛
Stevie Nicks（ˈstivɪ ˈnɪks）史蒂薇妮克斯
Whitney Houston（ˈhwɪtnɪ hjustn̩）惠妮休斯頓

☆　☆　☆　☆　☆　☆　☆　☆

Billy Joel（ˈbɪlɪ ˈdʒol）比利喬
Bob Dylan（ˈbɑb ˈdɪln̩）鮑布狄倫
Bryan Adams（ˈbraɪn̩ ˈædəmz）布萊恩亞當斯
Bruce Springsteen（ˈbrus ˈsprɪŋstɪn）布魯斯史普林斯汀
Chris De Burgh（ˈkrɪs də ˈbɝ）克里斯迪博夫
David Bowie（ˈdevɪd ˈboɪ）大衛鮑依
Elton John（ˈɛltən ˈdʒɑn）艾爾頓強
George Michael（ˈdʒɔrdʒ ˈmaɪkl̩）喬治邁克
Jon Secada（ˈdʒɑn səˈkɑdə）約翰史卡達
John Lennon（ˈdʒɑn ˈlɛnən）約翰藍儂
Michael Bolton（ˈmaɪkl̩ ˈboltn̩）麥可波頓
Michael Jackson（ˈmaɪkl̩ ˈdʒæksn̩）麥可傑克森
Paul McCartney（ˈpɔl məˈkɑrtnɪ）保羅麥卡尼
Paul Simon（ˈpɔl ˈsaɪmən）保羅賽門
Phil Collins（ˈfɪl ˈkɑlɪnz）菲爾柯林斯
Prince（prɪns）王子
Rod Stewart（ˈrɑd ˈstjuwə˞t）洛史都華
Sting（stɪŋ）史汀

4. Television 電 視

📞 *打電話問老師問題*

1. How much television do you watch？ 你看多少電視？

2 How many TV sets does your family have?
你家有幾台電視？

3. What television programs do you watch on a regular basis？
你通常收看什麼電視節目？

4. What is the state of television in Taiwan right now？
台灣目前的電視狀況如何？

5. Do you think television is a good or bad thing？
你認為電視是好或是壞？

6. Is the state of television in Taiwan pretty bad right now？
台灣當前的電視狀況眞的很糟嗎？

7. If you were in charge, what would you do to improve the
standard of television？
如果你是主管，你會如何來改善電視的水準？

8. Do you have a favorite program on TV？
你有最喜歡的電視節目嗎？

9. Do you watch cable television？ 你收看有線電視嗎？

10. What kind of influence do you think television has on
young people today？
你覺得電視對時下的年輕人有什麼影響？

📞 打電話和老師討論問題

Dialogue 1

老師： How much television do you watch?
你看多少電視？

學生： I used to watch a lot of television, but I don't watch much now for two reasons: one, I think most of the programs are poor and two, I don't have as much time as I used to.
我以前常看電視，不過我現在看得不多，原因有二：一、我覺得大部分的節目很差，二、我現在的時間沒有以前多。

老師： What television programs do you watch on a regular basis? 你通常收看什麼電視節目？

學生： I try to have the news on when I eat my supper, so I can *kill two birds with one stone*. Otherwise I tend to watch informative programs, and sometimes when there is a good movie on, I watch it.
我邊吃晚飯邊看新聞，這是一石二鳥之計。不然的話，我就看些知識性的節目。當電視播放好電影的時候，我也會收看。
→ informative (ɪnˈfɔrmətɪv) *adj.* 知識性的

老師： What is the state of television in Taiwan right now?
台灣目前的電視狀況如何？

學生： Taiwan has three domestic channels and cable television, which was legalized in 1993 although it existed illegally before then. A lot of people watch cable television because of its diversity.
台灣有三個國內頻道和有線電視，有線電視在 1993 年合法化，不過在之前就已非法存在。許多人收看有線電視，因為它的內容豐富。
→ domestic (dəˈmɛstɪk) *adj.* 國內的　　channel (ˈtʃænḷ) *n.* 頻道
diversity (dəˈvɝsətɪ , daɪ-) *n.* 變化

Dialogue 2

老師： Do you think television is a good or bad thing?
你認為電視是好或是壞？

學生： I think it is a wonderful invention which has vast potential, but isn't used to its full potential. There is far too much junk around, and the aim of a lot of the programs is "anything for a cheap laugh", which I think is pretty low.
我認為電視是項偉大的發明，它有廣大的潛力，只是未被充分發揮。我們擁有的是過多的垃圾，許多節目的目的只是「搏君一笑」，這在我看來真是低俗不堪。
➡ potential〔pə'tɛnʃəl〕 *n.* 潛力

老師： So are you saying that the state of television in Taiwan is pretty bad right now?
你言下之意是說台灣當前的電視狀況糟透了？

學生： There are both good and bad programs, but I think there are too many low quality, bad programs being broadcasted. Someone really should do something about that.
好、壞節目都有，但我認為有太多低水準的爛節目在播放。真該有人來管管這檔事。
➡ broadcast〔'brɔd͵kæst〕 *v.* 廣播；播放

老師： If you were in charge, what would you do to improve the standard of television?
如果你是主管，你會如何來改善電視的水準？

學生： I would, for a start, ax the low quality programs slowly. I would introduce high quality programs gradually so as to ease the viewers into it and eventually phase out all the bad programs.
首先，我會慢慢地削減低水準的節目，逐漸增加高品質的節目，讓觀眾逐步接受它們。最後，我會按階段剔除所有的爛節目。
➡ ax〔æks〕 *v.* 削減   *phase out* 分段廢除

Dialogue 3

老師： Do you have a favorite program on TV ?
你有最喜歡的電視節目嗎？

學生： I think my favorite program is "The X Files." It has an element of suspense and *taps into* one of the strongest of human desires: *curiosity for the unknown* and makes a great program from it.
我想我最喜歡的節目是「X檔案」。它含有懸疑的成份，觸動人類最最強烈的慾望之一：對未知的好奇心，並從中成就偉大事業。

老師： Do you watch cable television ?
你收看有線電視嗎？

學生： I have cable TV in my house, but I only watch the movie channel when there's a good movie on. Cable television is pretty widespread in Taiwan.
我家裝了有線電視，但是我只在有好電影時，才收看電影頻道。有線電視在台灣十分普遍。

老師： What kind of influence do you think television has on young people today ?
你覺得電視對時下的年輕人有什麼影響？

學生： That depends on which kinds of programs they watch. There are good programs that are beneficial and bad ones that corrupt the children. I think it is up to the parents whether their kids are watching good TV or not.
那要視他們收看的節目而定。電視提供有益的好節目，也有讓孩子墮落的壞節目。我認為那取決於父母是否讓小孩收看有益的電視節目。

**

element (ˈɛləmənt) *n.* 成份　　suspense (səˈspɛns) *n.* 懸疑
tap (tæp) *v.* 輕敲　　beneficial (ˌbɛnəˈfɪʃəl) *adj.* 有益的

節目類別

news & weather 新聞氣象
soap opera 連續劇
quiz show 猜謎節目
* quiz (kwɪz) *n.* 測驗題
contest show 比賽節目
interview show 訪問節目
variety show 綜藝節目
children's show 兒童節目
musical program 音樂節目
puppet show 布袋戲
 * puppet ('pʌpɪt) *n.* 木偶
Taiwanese opera 歌仔戲
live show 現場節目

giveaway 實況播出
satellite transmission 衛星轉播
* satellite ('sætḷ‚aɪt) *n.* 衛星
 transmission (træns'mɪʃən) *n.* 傳送
rerun 重播節目
prime time 黃金時段
promotional trailer 節目預告
* promotional (prə'moʃənḷ) *adj.* 宣傳的
 trailer ('trelə) *n.* 預告片
commercial (kə'mɝʃəl) *n.* 廣告
MC 主持人
 (= Master of Ceremonies)
Emmy Award 艾美獎
Golden Bell Award 金鐘獎

5. Reading 閱 讀

📞 打電話問老師問題

1. How much do you read these days？你目前閱讀多少東西？

2. What kinds of books do you read for recreation？
   你都讀什麼書作消遣？

3. Do you have any favorite authors？你有沒有喜歡的作家？

4. Why is Asimov your favorite science fiction author？
   為什麼你最喜歡的科幻小說作家是艾西蒙？

5. Do you have any other favorite authors？
   你還有其他喜歡的作家嗎？

6. How much reading do you do every day？
   你每天閱讀多少？

7. How many languages do you read on a regular basis？
   你通常都閱讀幾種語言的讀物？

8. Do you enjoy your reading？你喜歡閱讀嗎？

9. Are you going to be reading as often after you graduate？
   你畢業後還會經常閱讀嗎？

10. What is your favorite novel？你最喜歡的小說是那一本？

11. Why did you like it？你為什麼喜歡它？

12. How many novels have you read？你讀過多少小說？

📞 打電話和老師討論問題

Dialogue 1

老師：How much do you read these days?
你目前閱讀多少東西？

學生：The reading that I do is split into two parts: recreational and academic. For recreation I read newspapers, magazines and fictional books. For academic purposes I read textbooks and other reference books.
我所做的閱讀可分爲兩個部分：休閒娛樂與學術研究。我讀報紙、雜誌以及小說作爲消遣；讀教科書、參考書供作學術研究。

老師：What kinds of books do you read for recreation?
你都讀什麼書作消遣？

學生：I tend to read science fiction books because they take me away from this world into another dimension. I feel almost as if I were living in another world.
我大多讀科幻小說，因爲它們帶我遠離這個世界，進入另一度的空間，讓我彷彿置身另一個世界。

老師：Do you have any favorite science fiction authors?
你有沒有最喜歡的科幻小說家？

學生：I try to experiment and read all types of science fiction, but if I had to choose a favorite author, it would have to be the late Issac Asimov.
我盡量嘗試閱讀所有類型的科幻小說，不過若眞要我選一個最喜歡的小說家，應該是已故的艾撒克・艾西蒙。

** ────────────────────

academic (ˌækəˈdɛmɪk) *adj.* 學術的　　fictional (ˈfɪkʃənḷ) *adj.* 小說的
reference (ˈrɛfərəns) *n.* 參考書　　dimension (dəˈmɛnʃən) *n.* 空間；範圍

Dialogue 2

老師： Why is Asimov your favorite science fiction author?
為什麼艾西蒙是你最喜歡的科幻小說家？

學生： His books are the most intriguing of all the science fiction books I have read so far. In some of the books he wrote long ago, he was correct in predicting what would happen in the future.
在我讀過的所有科幻小說中，他的作品是最迷人的。一些很久以前的著作，都準確地預測出未來可能發生的事。

老師： Do you have any other favorite authors?
你還有其他喜歡的作家嗎？

學生： Sure. There is a book called "Wild Swans" which is by Chang Jung. It tells the story of three Chinese women in three different generations. I am still reading it, and I really like it so far.
當然。我喜歡張戎寫的「鴻」，它描述三個不同時代中國女性的一生。我現在正在讀，我真的好喜歡它。

老師： How much reading do you do every day?
你每天閱讀多少？

學生： I read textbooks during the day while in college, but *on the way to and from* college I tend to read Chinese fiction novels. And at night before I go to bed, I read magazines and newspapers.
白天在大學時，我看教科書，但在往返學校途中，我都看中文小說。晚上就寢前，我看雜誌和報紙。

**
intriguing (ɪn'trigɪŋ) adj. 有魅力的   swan (swɑn) n. 天鵝

Dialogue 3

老師： How many languages do you read on a regular basis ?
你通常都閱讀幾種語言的讀物？

學生： I read Chinese every day, and I read English almost every day. I want to improve my level of English, and I think reading is a very good way for me to achieve my goal. I read English newspapers and magazines.
我每天都會看中文，而英文幾乎也是天天看。我想提昇我的英文程度，我認為閱讀是達到目標的好方法。我都讀英文報紙和雜誌。

老師： Yes, I think reading is a good way of improving your English, too. Do you enjoy your reading ?
是的，我也認為閱讀是提昇你英文的好方法。你喜歡閱讀嗎？

學生： I like it. I think reading for recreation is a very good way for one to relax. Especially stories and novels. They really soothe the mind.
我喜歡。我認為消遣式的閱讀是放鬆心情的好辦法。尤其是故事和小說，它們的確能紓解你的心靈。

老師： Are you going to be reading as often after you graduate ?　你畢業後還會經常閱讀嗎？

學生： I think so. I think that even when I have started working, I'll still continue the hobby of reading. I think it is a good hobby, and I think I will *carry on with* it for the rest of my life!
我想是如此。我認為即使我開始工作，我還是會繼續閱讀的嗜好。我覺得這是個很好的嗜好，所以我會終生持續。

**

soothe〔suð〕*v.* 使安靜

文學類別

the classics 古典文學
contemporary literature 現代文學
* contemporary (kən'tɛmpə,rɛrɪ) adj. 現代的

poetry ('po·ɪtrɪ) 詩
comedy ('kamədɪ) 喜劇
melodrama ('mɛlə,dramə) 通俗劇
farce (fɑrs) 鬧劇
novel ('navḷ) 長篇小說
short story 短篇小說

drama ('dramə) 戲劇
tragedy ('trædʒədɪ) 悲劇

fiction ('fɪkʃən) 小說
novelette (,navḷ'ɛt) 中篇小說
nonfiction 非小說

❧ ❧ ❧ ❧ ❧ ❧ ❧ ❧ ❧ ❧

mystery ('mɪst(ə)rɪ) 怪誕故事；推理小說
whodunit (hu'dʌnɪt) 推理小說；偵探小說
detective story 偵探小說　* detective (dɪ'tɛktɪv) adj. 偵探的
historical novel 歷史小說
knight-errant novel 武俠小說　* knight-errant ('naɪt'ɛrənt) n. 遊俠騎士
science fiction 科幻小說
fairy tale 童話
mythology (mɪ'θɑlədʒɪ) 神話
autobiography (,ɔtəbaɪ'ɑgrəfɪ) 自傳

romance 羅曼史
fable ('febḷ) 寓言
biography (baɪ'ɑgrəfɪ) 傳記

❧ ❧ ❧ ❧ ❧ ❧ ❧ ❧ ❧

memoirs ('mɛmwɑrz) 回憶錄
prose (proz) 散文
bestseller 暢銷書
pirate book 盜版書　* pirate ('paɪrət) n. 侵害著作；海盜
anecdote ('ænɪk,dot) 軼事；逸聞
pseudonym ('sjudṇ,ɪm ,'su-) 筆名
anonymous (ə'nɑnəməs) 作者不詳的

essay ('ɛse) 隨筆
comic ('kamɪk) 漫畫
out of print 絕版

criticism ('krɪtə,sɪzṃ) 評論

☆ 知名作家 ☆

Alice Walker〔'ælɪs 'wɔkɚ〕艾麗斯渥克（美國小說家）

Amy Tan〔'æmɪ 'tɑn〕譚恩美（華裔美國小說家）

Anne Rice〔'æn 'raɪs〕安萊絲（美國小說家）

Arthur Miller〔'ɑrθɚ 'mɪlɚ〕亞瑟・米勒（美國劇作家）

Camus〔kɑ'mju〕卡繆（法國短篇小說家、劇作家、散文家）

Dostoevski〔,dostɔ'jɛfskɪ〕杜斯妥也夫斯基（俄國小說家）

Faulkner〔'fɔknɚ〕福克納（美國小說家）

Graham Greene〔'græm 'grin〕葛萊姆格林（英國小說家）

Gide〔ʒid〕紀德（法國小說家、批評家及散文家）

Hemingway〔'hɛmɪŋ,we〕海明威（美國小說家、記者）

Hesse〔'hɛsə〕赫塞（德國作家）

Hugo〔'hjugo〕雨果（法國詩人、小說家、劇作家）

📖　📖　📖　📖　📖

John Grisham〔'dʒɑn 'grɪʃæm〕約翰葛里遜（美國暢銷小說家）

John Updike〔'dʒɑn 'ʌpdaɪk〕約翰厄普戴克（美國暢銷小說家）

James Joyce〔'dʒæmz 'dʒɔɪs〕喬艾斯（愛爾蘭小說家）

Kazuo Ishiguru〔kɑ'zuo ɪʃɪ'guru〕石黑一雄（日裔英國暢銷小說家）

Mark Twain〔'mɑrk 'twen〕馬克吐溫（美國小說家及幽默家）

Michael Chriton〔'maɪkḷ 'kraɪtṇ〕米高克里頓（美國暢銷小說家）

Sartre〔'sɑrtrə〕沙特（法國哲學家、劇作家、小說家）

Shakespeare〔'ʃɛkspɪr〕莎士比亞（英國詩人、戲劇家）

Sidney Sheldon〔'sɪdnɪ 'ʃɛldṇ〕席尼薛爾頓（美國小說家）

Stephen King〔'stivən 'kɪŋ〕史蒂芬金（美國暢銷小說家）

Tom Clancy〔'tɑm 'klensɪ〕湯姆克蘭西（美國暢銷小說家）

Toni Morrison〔'tonɪ 'morɪsṇ〕東妮摩里森（美國小說家）

Tolstoy〔'tolstɔɪ〕托爾斯泰（俄國小說家、哲學家、神祕主義者）

T. S. Eliot〔'ɛljət〕艾略特（英國詩人及批評家）

Yeats〔jets〕葉慈（愛爾蘭詩人及劇作家）

6. *Traveling* 旅 遊

📞 *打電話問老師問題*

1. Do you like to travel？ 你喜歡旅行嗎？

2. Where do you like to travel to？ 你喜歡到那裏旅行？

3. Do you like to go on tours？ 你喜歡跟團旅行嗎？

4. Do you like to plan your own trip？
   你喜歡規劃自己的旅行嗎？

5. What is your favorite destination？
   你最喜歡的目的地是那裡？

6. What countries have you traveled to？
   你去過那些國家？

7. What was your best traveling experience？
   你最美好的旅遊經驗是什麼？

8. What was your worst traveling experience？
   你最慘的旅遊經驗是什麼？

9. Do you like to travel alone？ 你喜歡一個人旅行嗎？

10. What is your favorite time of year to travel？
    你最喜歡在什麼時節去旅行？

11. How often do you travel？ 你多久旅行一次？

12. Do you like to travel with friends？ 你喜歡和朋友一起旅行嗎？

📞 *打電話和老師討論問題*

Dialogue 1

老師：Do you like to travel？ 你喜歡旅行嗎？

學生：Of course. I usually travel during my holidays, and when I have free time, which is usually during the summer, I tend to travel abroad.
當然。當我放假時，我通常會去旅行，而有空閒的時候，通常是在夏天，我大多會到國外旅行。

老師：Where do you like to travel to？
你喜歡到那裡旅行？

學生：Well, I like to go to places which are scenic because they make me feel so relaxed. I suppose out of all the places that I have been to my favorite has to be Taroko gorge. It's magnificent.
我喜歡到風景勝地，因爲它們使我感到無比的自在。在我拜訪過的所有地方中，我想我最喜歡的就是太魯閣峽谷。它實在很壯觀。

老師：Do you like to go on tours？
你喜歡跟旅行團旅遊嗎？

學生：Not really. I don't like to be *herded around like sheep*. I would much prefer to travel with a bunch of friends. The only thing I like about traveling in groups is that *everything is taken care of*.
不是很喜歡。我不喜歡像羊一樣被人驅趕，我寧可和一夥朋友去旅行。團體旅遊唯一讓我喜歡的一點是，每件事都有人幫你照料好。

** ───────────

scenic (ˈsinɪk ˌˈsɛn-) *adj.* 風景的   gorge (gɔrdʒ) *n.* 峽谷
magnificent (mægˈnɪfəsn̩t) *adj.* 壯麗的   herd (hɝd) *v.* 使成群
bunch (bʌntʃ) *n.* 群

Dialogue 2

老師： Do you like to plan your own trip?
你喜歡規劃自己的旅行嗎?

學生： Yes! I think it's as enjoyable as traveling itself. You learn a lot by planning out all the details of your travels. I'd recommend all my friends to make their own travel arrangements.
是的!我認為那跟旅行本身同樣有趣。你可以從計畫旅遊細節中學到很多。我會建議所有的朋友自己來安排旅遊事宜。

老師： What is your favorite destination?
你最喜歡的目的地是那裡?

學生： I like Australia a lot because it's so big and there's such nice scenery. I like to see the cultural differences between the people in different countries.
我十分喜歡澳洲,因為它的領土廣闊、景色優美。我喜歡看各國人民間的文化差異。

老師： What countries have you traveled to?
你到那些國家旅行過?

學生： I've been to five countries *in all*, the USA, Australia, New Zealand, England and Japan. I like to travel in the summer because the weather is nice and you are *in good spirits* already.
我一共去過五個國家:美國、澳洲、紐西蘭、英國和日本。我喜歡在夏日時旅遊,因為天氣好,你的精神也為之振奮。

**
destination (ˏdɛstə'neʃən) n. 目的地
in all 合計

Dialogue 3

老師： What was your best traveling experience?
你最美好的旅遊經驗是什麼？

學生： It was when I went to San Francisco to visit my aunt last summer. My aunt showed me all the nice places to see in California. I went to Disneyland and Hollywood; it was most memorable.
就是我去年夏天到舊金山拜訪姑姑的那一次。姑姑帶我參觀加州所有的勝地，我去了狄斯耐樂園和好萊塢，那次旅行最令我難忘。

老師： What was your worst traveling experience?
你最慘的旅遊經驗是什麼？

學生： It would have to be the trip to Japan. I think it was mainly because I went on a tour, and we were hurried along. I didn't have any time on my own, and I think the goods were over-priced.
應該是日本之旅那一回。我想主要是因為我跟團旅遊，一路被趕著走，我沒有任何自己的時間。此外，我覺得那邊的東西價格過高。

老師： Do you like to travel alone?
你喜歡一個人旅行嗎？

學生： No, I prefer to travel with my friends. They are good company, and we can help each other. It is also cheaper to travel in a group, *as opposed to* traveling alone.
不，我較喜歡和朋友一起旅行。他們是很好的同伴，而且我們也可以彼此照應。此外，團體旅遊比單獨旅行來得便宜。

**

memorable (ˈmɛmərəbḷ) *adj.* 難忘的
opposed (əˈpozd) *adj.* 相對的

旅遊相關語彙

airport (ˈɛrˌport) *n.* 機場

customs (ˈkʌstəmz) *n. pl.* 海關

duty free shop 免稅商店

immigration (ˌɪməˈgreʃən) *n.* 入境

check in 入關登記

pilot (ˈpaɪlət) *n.* 駕駛員

stewardess (ˈstjuwədɪs) *n.* 空中小姐

control tower 塔台

tax 稅金

beverage (ˈbɛv(ə)rɪdʒ) *n.* 飲料

layover (ˈleˌovə) *n.* 暫時滯留

steward (ˈstjuwəd) *n.* 空中少爺

இ இ இ இ இ

flight attendant 空服員

business class 商務艙

travel agency 旅行社

baggage (ˈbægɪdʒ) *n.* 行李

frequent flyer 空中飛人

confirmation (ˌkanfəˈmeʃən) *n.* 確認

first class 頭等艙

economy coach 經濟艙

passenger (ˈpæsṇdʒə) *n.* 乘客

voucher (ˈvautʃə) *n.* 優待券

coupon (ˈkupan) *n.* 回數票；折價券

環遊世界

Argentina (ˌardʒənˈtinə) 阿根廷

Austria (ˈɔstrɪə) 奧地利

Belgium (ˈbɛldʒəm) 比利時

Canada (ˈkænədə) 加拿大

Cuba (ˈkjubə) 古巴

Czechoslovakia (ˌtʃɛkəsloˈvækɪə) 捷克

Denmark (ˈdɛnˌmark) 丹麥

Fiji (ˈfidʒi) 斐濟

France (fræns , frans) 法國

Greece (gris) 希臘

Australia (ɔˈstreljə) 澳大利亞

Bahamas (bəˈhaməz) 巴哈馬

Brazil (brəˈzɪl) 巴西

Colombia (kəˈlʌmbɪə) 哥倫比亞

Cyprus (ˈsaɪprəs) 賽普勒斯

Egypt (ˈidʒɪpt) 埃及

Finland (ˈfɪnlənd) 芬蘭

Germany (ˈdʒəmənɪ) 德國

Guam (gwam) 關島

Hong Kong（'haŋ 'kaŋ）香港
India（'ɪndɪə）印度
Ireland（'aɪrlənd）愛爾蘭
Japan（dʒə'pæn）日本
Luxembourg（'lʌksəm,bɝg）盧森堡
Macao（mə'kaʊ）澳門
Malta（'mɔltə）馬爾他
Monaco（'manə,ko）摩納哥
Morocco（mə'rako）摩洛哥

Iceland（'aɪslənd）冰島
Indonesia（,ɪndə'niʃə, -ʒə）印尼
Italy（'ɪtəlɪ）義大利
South Korea（saʊθ ko'riə）南韓

Malaysia（mə'leʒə, -ʃə）馬來西亞
Mexico（'mɛksɪ,ko）墨西哥
Mongolia（maŋ'golɪə）外蒙古
Nepal（nɪ'pɔl）尼泊爾

🐌 🐌 🐌 🐌 🐌 🐌 🐌

Netherlands（'nɛðəələndz）荷蘭
New Zealand（nju'zilənd）紐西蘭
Norway（'nɔr,we）挪威
Panama（'pænə,ma）巴拿馬
Portugal（'portʃəgl̩）葡萄牙
Puerto Rico（,pwɛrtə'riko）波多黎各
Saudi Arabia（sɑ'udɪ ə'rebɪə）沙烏地阿拉伯
Singapore（'sɪŋgə,por）新加坡
South Africa（saʊθ 'æfrɪkə）南非

Palau（pə'laʊ）帛琉
Philippines（'fɪlə,pinz）菲律賓

🐌 🐌 🐌 🐌 🐌 🐌 🐌

Spain（spen）西班牙
Switzerland（'swɪtsəələnd）瑞士
Thailand（'taɪlənd）泰國
United Kingdom（ju'naɪtɪd 'kɪŋdəm）英國
United States（ju'naɪtɪd 'stets）美國
Vatican（'vætɪkən）梵蒂岡
Venezuela（,vɛnə'zwilə）委內瑞拉
Vietnam（,viɛt'nɑm）越南

Sweden（'swidn̩）瑞典
Tahiti（tɑ'hiti）大溪地
Turkey（'tɝkɪ）土耳其

28

7. Shopping　購物

📞 *打電話問老師問題*

1. Do you like to go shopping？ 你喜歡逛街買東西嗎？

2. Where do you like to go shopping？ 你喜歡去那逛街買東西？

3. Do you pay attention to prices when you go shopping？
   逛街買東西時，你會注意價錢嗎？

4. Do you like to bargain for lower prices？ 你喜歡殺價嗎？

5. Do you think that it is important to buy products of
   high quality？ 你覺得購買高品質的產品很重要嗎？

6. When was the last time you went shopping？
   你最近一次去逛街買東西是什麼時候？

7. What did you buy？ 你買了什麼？

8. How much money did you spend？ 你花了多少錢？

9. How often do you go shopping？ 你多常去逛街買東西？

10. What do you like to shop for？ 你喜歡逛街買什麼東西？

11. Do you wait to buy products when they are on sale？
    你會等拍賣時才去買東西嗎？

12. Do you shop around and compare prices at different
    stores？ 你會四處逛逛，而且比較不同商店的價錢嗎？

📞 *打電話和老師討論問題*

Dialogue 1

老師： Do you like to go shopping?
你喜歡逛街買東西嗎？

學生： Yes, shopping is one of my favorite things to do.
Most of my salary is spent on shopping.
是的。逛街買東西是我最喜歡做的事情之一，我大部分的薪水都花
在買東西上。

老師： Where do you like to go shopping?
你喜歡去那逛街買東西？

學生： My favorite place for shopping is the night market. I
also like to shop at department stores.
我最喜歡的購物地點是夜市。我也喜歡在百貨公司買東西。

老師： Why do you like to go shopping at the night market?
你為什麼喜歡在夜市買東西？

學生： I like to shop at the night market because the prices
there are very low. I also like to look at the many
different clothes, purses, jewelry and watches that they
sell at the night market.
我喜歡在夜市買東西，因為那兒的價格很低。我也喜歡看夜市賣的
許多不同的衣服、皮包、珠寶以及手錶。

** ————————————————————————
salary (ˈsælərɪ) *n.* 薪水　　*night market* 夜市
purse (pɝs) *n.* 皮包　　jewelry (ˈdʒuəlrɪ) *n.* 珠寶

Dialogue 2

老師： Do you pay attention to prices when you go shopping？
逛街買東西時，你會注意價錢嗎？

學生： Of course. I always shop around at different stores to find the lowest price.
當然。我總是在不同的商店四處逛，以找到最低的價格。

老師： Do you like to bargain for a lower price？
你喜歡殺價嗎？

學生： Yes. It's fun to bargain. And if you don't bargain, you can't get the best price.
是啊，殺價很有趣。而且如果你不殺價，就不會得到最好的價格。

老師： Do you think it's important to buy products of high quality？
你覺得購買高品質的產品很重要嗎？

學生： It depends on the product. I pay attention to quality when I buy expensive things, such as electronic products. For everyday items, I just look for the lowest price.
這要看是什麼產品。購買昂貴的東西，像是電器產品時，我會注意品質。至於日常用品，我只找價格最低的。

**
―――――――――――――――

bargain (ˈbɑrgɪn) *v.* 討價還價　　***depend on*** 視～而定
electronic (ɪ͵lɛkˈtrɑnɪk) *adj.* 電子的　　item (ˈaɪtəm) *n.* 項目；細目

Dialogue 3

老師： When was the last time you went shopping ?
你上次去逛街買東西是什麼時候？

學生： Last weekend. I went to the department store with my friends.
上個週末。我和朋友到百貨公司去。

老師： What did you buy ?
你買了什麼？

學生： I bought a pair of shoes, a shirt and a scarf.
我買了一雙鞋，一件襯衫和一條圍巾。

老師： How much money did you spend ?
你花了多少錢？

學生： Not very much. The department store was *having a sale*. I bought the shoes for 30% off, the shirt for 50% off, and the scarf only cost me 200 dollars.
沒有很多。百貨公司在大減價，我買的鞋子打七打，襯衫五折，而圍巾只花了我兩百元而已。

** ——————

scarf (skɑrf) *n.* 圍巾

8. *Cooking* 烹飪

📞 *打電話問老師問題*

1. Can you cook？ 你會做菜嗎？

2. Do you like to cook？ 你喜歡烹飪嗎？

3. Is it easy to find ingredients in Taiwan？
   在台灣找材料容易嗎？

4. Do you need a recipe to cook？ 你做菜需要看食譜嗎？

5. Do you like to cook for family and friends？
   你喜歡為家人和朋友燒菜嗎？

6. How did you learn to cook？ 你如何學做菜？

7. Does cooking come naturally to you？
   做菜對你來說是順理成章的事嗎？

8. What is the largest number of people you have cooked
   for at one time？ 你曾經最多一次煮飯給多少人吃？

9. What is your specialty？ 你的招牌菜是什麼？

10. What was the first thing you cooked？
    你煮的第一道菜是什麼？

11. Where do you go to buy ingredients for cooking in
    Taiwan？ 在台灣，你都到那裡買烹飪材料？

12. Can you cook gourmet food？ 你會烹調美食嗎？

📞 *打電話和老師討論問題*

Dialogue 1

老師： Can you cook?
你會做菜嗎?

學生： Of course. Even though I don't get a lot of time at home, I still *make the most of* the time that I have left.
當然。雖然我在家的時間不多,但依然充分利用剩餘的時間。

老師： Do you like to cook?
你喜歡烹飪嗎?

學生： Yes. It's actually an enjoyment. When I cook, I try to relax and enjoy myself as much as I can. Cooking is *a form of art*, and I like to experiment, too.
喜歡。事實上烹飪是種樂趣,當我做菜的時候,我會盡量放鬆心情,好好享受樂趣。烹飪是一種藝術,我也喜歡作實驗。

老師： Is it easy to find ingredients in Taiwan?
在台灣找材料容易嗎?

學生： Ingredients are everywhere in Taiwan! There are so many markets and supermarkets, *you can't miss them*. The important thing is to make sure that the food you buy is fresh and clean, though. I normally buy from the supermarket.
台灣到處都有材料!市場和超級市場那麼多,你不會找不著的。但是最重要是確保你買的食物新鮮且衛生。我通常都在超級市場購買。

** ————————

make the most of 充分利用　　ingredient〔ɪnˈgridɪənt〕*n.* 材料

Dialogue 2

老師：Do you need a recipe to cook？
你做菜需要看食譜嗎？

學生：Only if I'm trying out something new, which is not that often. I cook every day, so normally I don't need a recipe to cook. Also, I don't always agree with the recipe as my taste may differ with that of the author.
只有在嘗試新料理的時候才需要，不過我不常如此。我每天下廚，所以通常不需要靠食譜。此外，我也不完全贊同食譜的做法，因為我的口味可能和作者不一樣。

老師：Do you like to cook for family and friends？
你喜歡為家人和朋友做菜嗎？

學生：I like to, but I'm just an *average cook*. I *prefer to* take my friends out *rather than* to cook for them. As for my family, well, I cook for them normally, and we go out only during weekends or special occasions.
我喜歡烹飪，不過我的手藝普通，所以我寧願帶朋友到外面吃。至於我的家人，我大多會為他們下廚，只有在週末或特殊的場合，我們才到外頭吃飯。

老師：How did you learn to cook？ 你如何學做菜？

學生：At school we had cooking classes, so that's when I first started cooking. But I also helped my mother cook when I was a kid. My first dish was *egg fried rice*, and to this day it's still my best dish!
在學校的時候我們有烹飪課，我就是從那時起開始做菜。不過當我還小的時候，也幫過媽媽煮飯。我煮的第一道菜是蛋炒飯，到現在為止，它還是我最拿手的佳餚。

**————

recipe (ˈrɛsəpɪ, -pɪ) *n.* 食譜

Dialogue 3

老師： Does cooking come naturally to you?
做菜對你來說是順理成章的事嗎？

學生： In a way I've learned to *get used to* it. Nowadays it's relatively easy, and I enjoy cooking very much.
就某方面來說，我已經學著去習慣它。對我而言，做菜現在是輕而易舉，我也樂在其中。

老師： What is the largest number of people you have cooked for at one time?
你曾經最多一次煮飯給多少人吃？

學生： Roughly 10 people. It was New Year and I decided to cook for my friends as a special treat.
大概是十人。那時是新年，所以我決定下廚招待朋友。

I cooked about 10 dishes and surprisingly, my friends *cleaned the table*!
我煮了約十道菜，出人意外地，朋友們將之一掃而空。

老師： Out of all the countries, which style of cuisine is your favorite?
全世界的美食中，你最喜歡那一種？

學生： I think it would have to be French cuisine because I love the variety it offers. I am also a great fan of cheese and wine.
我想應該是法國菜，因為我喜歡它的變化多端，此外，我也非常熱愛起司和葡萄酒。

**

cuisine〔kwɪˈzin〕*n.* 美食；烹調   variety〔vəˈraɪətɪ〕*n.* 變化
fan〔fæn〕*n.* 迷

美食廣場

宮保雞丁　chicken with dry red pepper
蠔油牛肉　beef with oyster sauce　* oyster (ˈɔɪstɚ) *n.* 牡蠣
糖醋排骨　sweet and sour spareribs　* sparerib (ˈspɛr͵rɪb) *n.* 豬排骨
醋溜黃魚　yellow fish with sweet and sour sauce
蝦仁腰果　shrimp with cashew nuts　* cashew (ˈkæʃu, kəˈʃu) *n.* 腰果
茄汁明蝦　prawn with tomato sauce　* prawn (prɔn) *n.* 明蝦
醉雞　wined chicken
豆瓣魚　fish with hot bean sauce
奶油白菜　cabbage with cream sauce　* cabbage (ˈkæbədʒ) *n.* 包心菜
乾扁四季豆　fried string beans　* string (strɪŋ) *n.* 纖維；筋
麻婆豆腐　Ma-po's bean curd　* curd (kɝd) *n.* 凝乳
芥蘭牛肉　beef with broccoli　* broccoli (ˈbrɑk(ə)lɪ) *n.* 芥蘭菜

ᘉ　　　ᘉ　　　ᘉ

蛋花湯　egg drop soup
酸辣湯　hot and sour soup
雞茸玉米湯　minced chicken and corn soup　* mince (mɪns) *v.* 剁碎
家常菜　home-made dish
水餃　boiled dumplings　* dumpling (ˈdʌmplɪŋ) *n.* 蒸煮的麵糰
鍋貼　fried dumplings
春捲　spring rolls
蔥油餅　green onion pie

ᘉ　　　ᘉ　　　ᘉ

煙燻鮭魚　smoked salmon　* salmon (ˈsæmən) *n.* 鮭魚
義大利肉醬麵　spaghetti (spəˈgɛtɪ)
通心粉　macaroni (͵mækəˈronɪ)
德國豬腳　einsbein (ˈaɪnzbaɪn)　　披薩　pizza (ˈpitsə)
咖哩飯　curry and rice　　　　　　牛排　steak (stek)
羅宋湯　borsch (bɔrʃ)　　　　　　香腸　sausage (ˈsɔsɪdʒ)

9. Fast Food 速食

📞 *打電話問老師問題*

1. How much fast food do you consume in a week?
   你一個星期吃多少速食?

2. What type of fast food do you eat? 你吃那種速食?

3. Why do you think you eat so much fast food?
   你想為什麼你吃這麼多速食?

4. Do you think fast food is a good or bad thing?
   你覺得速食是好還是不好?

5. If fast food restaurants increased prices and improved their food, would customers be more satisfied?
   如果速食店提高售價並改善食物,顧客會比較滿意嗎?

6. Do you have a favorite fast food?
   你有沒有最喜歡的速食呢?

7. What type of fast food do you prefer, Eastern or Western?
   你比較喜歡那種速食,西式還是中式?

8. Would you do anything to change the fast food industry as it stands?
   就現狀而言,你會做什麼來改變速食業嗎?

9. What do you think the future of fast food will be?
   你認為速食的前景如何?

📞 *打電話和老師討論問題*

Dialogue 1

老師： How much fast food do you consume in a week?
你一個星期吃多少速食？

學生： I am always eating fast food when I am out. I'd say I eat fast food nearly once a day. It's bad for me, I know, but I don't have much of a choice.
我出門在外時都吃速食，可以說我幾乎每天都吃一次速食。我知道這對我不好，但我沒多少選擇。

老師： What type of fast food do you eat?
你吃那種速食？

學生： When I say fast food, I mean everything from hamburgers from McDonald's to Chinese pork buns from a stand.
當我說到速食時，我是指從麥當勞的漢堡，到小攤子所賣的中式肉包之類的所有東西。

They are all essentially the same, food which is served fast and taken fast, for people who are *in a hurry*.
它們本質上全都相同，都是快速供應、快速拿取的食物，提供給那些匆忙的人們。

**

consume〔kən'sum, -'sjum〕v. 消費；消耗
pork〔pork〕n. 豬肉　　bun〔bʌn〕n. 小圓麵包
essentially〔ə'sɛnʃəlɪ〕adv. 本質上

老師：Why do you think you eat so much fast food?
你想為什麼你吃這麼多速食？

學生：I think it is because *the pace in Taiwan is so fast*. Everyone is always in a hurry, and they don't have time to eat properly. This is especially true for students, who get very little time as they have to go to cram schools !
我想是因為台灣的步調如此快速，每個人總是很匆忙，沒有時間好好地吃一頓飯。這種情形尤其發生在學生身上，因為必須去補習班，所以時間很少。

Dialogue 2

老師：Do you think fast food is a good or a bad thing ?
你覺得速食是好還是不好？

學生：I would say that it is bad for your health, but it is a useful thing. I don't think most people could survive without it.
我會說對你的健康不好，但很方便。我想大部分的人不能沒有它。

老師：If the fast food restaurants raised their prices and made their food better, would customers be more satisfied ?
如果速食店提高售價並改善食物，顧客會比較滿意嗎？

學生：Not really. People these days are not too concerned with the flavor of the food, just the price of the food !
不見得，現在的人不太在意食物的口味，只關心食物的價錢。

**

pace〔pes〕*n.* 步調　　survive〔sə'vaɪv〕*v.* 存活
customer〔'kʌstəmə〕*n.* 顧客　　*be concerned with* 關心；關切

老師： Do you have a favorite fast food?
你有沒有最喜歡的速食呢？

學生： I would have to *go with* McDonald's since I've been eating there for many years, and I'm just used to the style of food they offer.
旣然我在麥當勞吃了許多年，我就必須適應，而且我也習慣他們所提供的食物。

Dialogue 3

老師： What type of fast food do you prefer, Eastern or Western?
你比較喜歡那種速食，西式還是中式？

學生： I prefer Western food, which may sound strange since I am Chinese. The restaurants which sell Western food are cleaner and are more common than the Eastern ones, so I prefer them.
我偏愛西式食物，這聽起來可能有點奇怪，因爲我是中國人。但是賣西式食物的餐廳較乾淨，而且比中式的普遍，所以我偏好西式。

老師： Would you do anything to change the fast food industry as it stands?
就現狀而言，你會做什麼來改變速食業嗎？

學生： I think there is always *room for improvement*, but the restaurants are doing a fairly good job as it is. The shops are clean, and they *project a clean image*.
我認爲總是有改善的空間，但是這些餐廳現在已相當不錯了。店面很乾淨，而且樹立乾淨的形象。

** ───────────────────────
go with 與～調和；適合　　*as it stands* 就現在的情形來說
project〔prə'dʒɛkt〕*v.* 投射出

老師：What do you think the future of fast food will be？
你認為速食的前景如何？

學生：I think there will be more and more fast food because of the increase in population and also the increase in people eating out. I hope there will be more nutritious fast food in the future！
由於人口的增加，以及外食的人數增多，我想會有愈來愈多的速食。我希望將來會有較多營養的速食。

─────────────────

nutritious (nju'trɪʃəs) *adj.* 有營養的

10. Vegetarianism 素食

☎ 打電話問老師問題

1. Are you a vegetarian? 你吃素嗎?

2. Have you ever tried to be a vegetarian before?
你以前曾經試過吃素嗎?

3. Do you think a vegetarian diet is bland?
你認爲素菜平淡無味嗎?

4. Do you think it is easier for vegetarians to stay thin?
你認爲吃素比較容易保持苗條嗎?

5. Do you think it is difficult for vegetarians to get enough
nutrients in their diets?
你認爲素食者的飲食很難得到足夠的營養嗎?

6. Do you think being a vegetarian is good for your
health? 你認爲吃素有益健康嗎?

7. Do you think it is wrong to eat animals?
你認爲吃動物的肉不對嗎?

8. Do you think there is a difference between eating meat
and eating dairy products or eggs?
你認爲吃肉類食物和吃乳製品或蛋有差別嗎?

9. Does your religion promote vegetarianism?
你所信仰的宗教提倡吃素嗎?

10. Are any of your friends or family members vegetarians?
你的朋友或家人中有人吃素嗎?

📞 *打電話和老師討論問題*

Dialogue 1

老師：Are you a vegetarian？　你吃素嗎？

學生：No, I am not. I like to eat meat too much.
不，我不吃素，我太喜歡吃肉了。

老師：Have you ever tried to be a vegetarian before？
你以前曾經試過吃素嗎？

學生：Yes, a few years ago. I ate no meat for only a few weeks, but then Chinese New Year arrived, and I ate a lot of meat.
有，幾年前試過，但只持續了幾星期。然後農曆過年一到，我又吃了好多肉。

老師：Do you think a vegetarian diet is bland？
你認為素菜平淡無味嗎？

學生：I don't think so. There are a lot of good vegetarian restaurants that make delicious food.
我不這麼認為，有很多不錯的素食餐廳，菜都很好吃。

Dialogue 2

老師：Do you think it's easier for vegetarians to stay thin？
你認為吃素比較容易保持苗條嗎？

學生：Yes, I do. I've never seen a fat vegetarian.
是的，我從未見過肥胖的素食者。

＊＊ ─────────────────────────────────

vegetarian（ˌvɛdʒə'tɛrɪən）*n.* 素食者　　　bland（blænd）*adj.* 清淡的；溫和的

老師：Do you think it's difficult for vegetarians to get enough nutrients in their diets?

你認為素食者的飲食很難得到足夠的營養嗎？

學生：I think it depends on whether they eat *dairy products* or eggs. If they do not eat any meat, dairy products or eggs, I think they might not get enough protein and other nutrients.

我想這要取決於他們吃不吃乳製品或蛋。如果他們肉類、乳製品或蛋都不吃，那我認為，他們可能就無法得到足夠的蛋白質，以及其他的營養。

老師：Do you think being a vegetarian is good for your health? 你認為吃素有益健康嗎？

學生：I think it can be good for your health. I've heard that eating too much meat can be very unhealthy. People who consume too much meat tend to get gout and hypertension.

我想可能有益健康。我聽說吃太多肉對健康很不好，肉吃太多的人容易得痛風和高血壓。

Dialogue 3

老師：Do you think it is wrong to eat animals?

你認為吃動物的肉不對嗎？

學生：No, I do not think there's anything wrong with eating meat. But I do not like to think about it too much.

不，我不認為吃肉有什麼錯，不過我不喜歡想太多。

**

nutrient (ˈnjutrɪənt , ˈnu-) *n.* 營養物　　diet (ˈdaɪət) *n.* 飲食
depend on 視～而定　　dairy (ˈdɛrɪ) *adj.* 酪農的
dairy product 乳製品　　protein (ˈprotiɪn) *n.* 蛋白質
gout (gaʊt) *n.* 痛風　　hypertension (ˌhaɪpɚˈtɛnʃən) *n.* 高血壓

老師： Do you think there is a difference between eating meat and eating dairy products or eggs ?
你認爲吃肉類食物和吃乳製品或蛋有差別嗎？

學生： Definitely. No animals suffer if you eat dairy products or eggs.
當然有，如果吃乳製品或蛋，那動物就不用受苦了。

老師： Does your religion promote vegetarianism ?
你所信仰的宗教提倡吃素嗎？

學生： There are two days each month when we *are not supposed to* eat meat, as well as a few special festival days during the year.
每個月裡有兩天，每年也有一些特殊的節日，我們會吃素。

**──────

definitely (ˈdɛfənɪtlɪ) *adv.* 一定地；確定地
promote (prəˈmot) *v.* 提倡　　*be supposed to* 應該
as well as 以及　　festival (ˈfɛstəvl) *adj.* 節日的

11. Sleep 睡眠

打電話問老師問題

1. How long do you sleep each night？ 你每天晚上睡多久？

2. What time do you usually go to bed？ 你通常幾點睡覺？

3. Do you have trouble falling asleep？
   你有失眠的煩惱嗎？

4. Do you wake up in the middle of the night？
   你會在半夜醒來嗎？

5. Do you take a nap every day？ 你每天都有小睡嗎？

6. Do you talk in your sleep？ 你會說夢話嗎？

7. Do you dream at night？ 你晚上會作夢嗎？

8. Do you remember your dreams？ 你記得的夢嗎？

9. What position do you find is most comfortable to sleep,
   on your back, side or stomach？
   你覺得什麼睡姿最舒服，仰臥、側睡或趴著睡？

10. Are you a heavy sleeper？ 你睡得很沉嗎？

11. How many hours of sleep do you need？
    你需要幾小時的睡眠？

12. What kind of bed do you have？ 你的床是什麼樣的？

📞 *打電話和老師討論問題*

Dialogue 1

老師： How long do you sleep each night?
你每天晚上睡多久？

學生： I need a lot of sleep, usually about 9 hours per night. However, I seldom get enough sleep because I have too many things to do. So I get about 7 hours of sleep a night.
我需要很多睡眠，通常每晚要睡九小時左右。然而，我很少有機會獲得足夠的睡眠，因為我有太多事情得做。所以，我一個晚上大概睡七小時。

老師： What time do you usually go to bed?
你通常幾點睡？

學生： I go to bed around one every night, and I get up around eight. I am a fairly *heavy sleeper*, and I always have two alarm clocks ready to make sure that I get up on time!
我每晚約一點的時候睡，八點左右起床。我睡得很沈，所以總要準備兩個鬧鐘，才能讓自己準時起床。

老師： Do you have trouble falling asleep?
你有失眠的煩惱嗎？

學生： Generally speaking, no. But sometimes I get excited about something and I can't *get myself to fall asleep*, for example, the night before a major test.
大體說來，沒有。不過，有時候因為對某件事感到很興奮，便無法入眠。比方說，在大考的前一天晚上。

** ————————————————

seldom (ˈsɛldəm) *adv.* 很少　　*alarm clock* 鬧鐘

Dialogue 2

老師： Do you wake up in the middle of the night?
你會在半夜醒來嗎？

學生： Only if I have a nightmare! I'm happy to say that it is not too often. As I've said, I'm a pretty heavy sleeper, but nevertheless I sometimes get woken up by phone calls.
只有當我做惡夢的時候才會！不過很慶幸，這不常發生。我說過，我睡得相當熟，但是我偶爾還是會被電話吵醒。

老師： Do you take a nap every day?
你每天都有小睡嗎？

學生： Whenever I have spare time, I will take a little nap. Normally this is during lunchtime. It helps to *relieve some of the stress* I have from the morning.
每當有空閒時，通常是在午餐時間，我會小睡片刻。這有助於減輕我早上累積的壓力。

老師： Do you talk in your sleep?
你會說夢話嗎？

學生： I've been told that I talk in my sleep, but I never remember it. So I'm still doubtful as to whether I really do talk in my sleep. Actually I've been told that I snore too, but again I'm pretty doubtful about that.
有人告訴過我，我會說夢話，可是我都不記得。所以，我還是很懷疑自己是否真的說了夢話。其實也有人說我會打鼾，但同樣的，我對此也感到很懷疑。

** —————

nightmare（ˈnaɪt͵mɛr）n. 惡夢　　spare（spɛr）adj. 剩餘的
nap（næp）n. 小睡　　relieve（rɪˈliv）v. 減輕
stress（strɛs）n. 壓力；緊張　　snore（snor）v. 打鼾

Dialogue 3

老師： Do you dream at night？
你晚上會作夢嗎？

學生： I know that everyone dreams every night, but I rarely remember any of my dreams. Dreams are special, and I sometimes have the feeling of deja vu when I remember my dreams.
我知道每個人每天晚上都會作夢，但我很少記得自己的夢。夢很特別，當我想起自己的夢時，有時會有種似曾相識的感覺。

老師： Do you remember any of your dreams？
你記得任何你的夢嗎？

學生： Strangely enough, I remember more nightmares than dreams. I think *nightmares are much more impressive than dreams*. My nightmares normally consist of me falling down some cliff or waterfall！
很奇怪，我記得的惡夢比其他的夢更多。我想惡夢比一般夢，更讓人記憶深刻。在惡夢中，我常會從懸崖或瀑布掉下來。

老師： What position do you find is most comfortable to sleep, on your back, side or stomach？
你覺得什麼姿勢睡覺最舒服，仰臥、側睡或趴著睡？

學生： I tend to fall asleep on my side, but when I wake up, I'm always in a different position. I think it's because of the different dreams I've had during the course of the night.
我通常在側臥時入睡，但是當我醒來時，總是變成另一個睡姿。我想這是因為我在晚上睡覺時，做了不同的夢的緣故。

**

deja vu (ˌdeʒə'vju) *n.* 似曾相識
impressive (ɪm'prɛsɪv) *adj.* 令人印象深刻的　　cliff (klɪf) *n.* 懸崖

睡眠相關語彙

repose〔rɪˋpoz〕*n.* 休息；睡眠
slumber〔ˋslʌmbɚ〕*n.* 睡眠
doze〔doz〕*v. n.* 小睡
nap〔næp〕*n.* 小睡
siesta〔sɪˋɛstə〕*n.* 午睡
insomnia〔ɪnˋsɑmnɪə〕*n.* 失眠
nightmare〔ˋnaɪt͵mɛr〕*n.* 惡夢
sleep-walking 夢遊
snore〔snor〕*v.* 打鼾
drowsy〔ˋdraʊzɪ〕*adj.* 昏昏欲睡的
yawn〔jɔn〕*v.* 打呵欠
nod〔nɑd〕*v. n.* 打盹
single bed 單人床
double bed 雙人床
queen size bed 60吋大床
king size bed 72吋大床
sofa〔ˋsofə〕*n.* 沙發
brass bed 銅床
　* brass〔bræs〕*n.* 黃銅
water bed 水床

bunk bed 雙層床
crib〔krɪb〕*n.* 嬰兒床
mattress〔ˋmætrɪs〕*n.* 床墊
straw mattress 榻榻米
bedspread〔ˋbɛd͵sprɛd〕*n.* 床單
blanket〔ˋblæŋkɪt〕*n.* 毛毯
quilt〔kwɪlt〕*n.* 棉被
pillow〔ˋpɪlo〕*n.* 枕頭
dresser〔ˋdrɛsɚ〕*n.* 梳粧檯
night stand 床頭几
nightgown 睡衣
pajamas〔pəˋdʒæməz〕*n.* 睡衣
sleeping pill 安眠藥
caffeine〔ˋkæfi(ɪ)n〕*n.* 咖啡因
box-spring 彈簧墊中之圓柱彈簧
night-owl 夜貓子
　* owl〔aʊl〕*n.* 貓頭鷹
stay up；sit up 熬夜
burn the midnight oil 熬夜
toss and turn 輾轉難眠

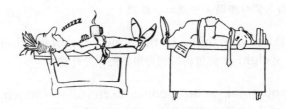

12. *Losing Weight* 減 肥

📞 *打電話問老師問題*

1. Have you ever tried to lose weight?
   你嘗試過減肥嗎？

2. Do you think it is easy to lose weight?
   你覺得減肥容易嗎？

3. What would you do to lose weight?
   你會怎麼減肥？

4. Do you think diets help people lose weight?
   你覺得吃減肥餐有助於減肥嗎？

5. Do you think exercise helps people lose weight?
   你覺得運動有助於減肥嗎？

6. How would you help a friend lose weight?
   你會如何幫助朋友減肥？

7. Do you think it's important for people to be thin?
   你覺得瘦對人們來說很重要嗎？

8. When do you think people should try to lose weight?
   你覺得人們什麼時候應該試著減肥？

9. What do you think is the most important thing to do to lose weight? 你覺得減肥最重要的事是什麼？

10. Do you think some people exercise too much to try to lose weight? 你是否覺得有些人為了試著減肥，而運動過量呢？

📞 *打電話和老師討論問題*

Dialogue 1

老師：Have you ever tried to lose weight?
你嘗試過減肥嗎？

學生：No. I'm fortunate to be naturally thin. But some of my friends try to lose weight even though they are not fat at all.
沒有。我很幸運天生就很瘦。但是儘管我有些朋友一點也不胖，他們也試著要減肥。

老師：Do you think it is easy to lose weight?
你覺得減肥容易嗎？

學生：I don't think it's easy to lose weight. I think losing weight requires a lot of self-discipline.
我覺得減肥不容易。我覺得減肥需要很大的自制力。

老師：What would you do to lose weight?
你會怎麼減肥？

學生：If I wanted to lose weight, I would try to exercise every day and eat only healthy foods.
如果我要減肥，我會試著每天運動，而且只吃健康食品。

** ────────────

lose weight 減肥；減輕體重 　*not at all* 一點也不
require (rɪ'kwaɪr) *v.* 需要
self-discipline ('sɛlf'dɪsəplɪn) *n.* 自律

Dialogue 2

老師 : Do you think diets help people lose weight?
你覺得減肥餐有助於減肥嗎？

學生 : Yes, I think diets can help people lose weight, but people should *consult doctors* before they do it.
是的，我覺得減肥餐能幫助減肥，但是在做之前，應該先請教醫生。

老師 : Do you think exercise helps people lose weight?
你覺得運動有助於減肥嗎？

學生 : Definitely. I think exercise is even more important than dieting, to help people lose weight.
當然。要幫助減肥，我覺得運動比吃減肥餐更重要。

老師 : How would you help a friend lose weight?
你會如何幫助朋友減肥？

學生 : I would encourage him or her to exercise regularly, perhaps by exercising with me.
我會鼓勵他規律地運動，也許可以和我一起運動。

Dialogue 3

老師 : Do you think it's important for people to be thin?
你覺得瘦對人們來說很重要嗎？

學生 : I think it's important for people to be healthy. Overweight people often have more health problems.
我覺得健康對人們來說很重要。過胖的人常常有較多的健康問題。

** ————————————————

diet (ˈdaɪət) *n. v.* 飲食；控制飲食　consult (kənˈsʌlt) *v.* 請教
definitely (ˈdɛfənɪtlɪ) *adv.* 當然；一定地
regularly (ˈrɛgjələlɪ) *adv.* 規律地；定期地
overweight (ˈovəˈwet) *adj.* 過胖的

老師：When do you think people should try to lose weight？
　　　你覺得什麼時候人們應該試著減肥？

學生：I think people should try to lose weight when their
　　　doctors tell them that they should, or when they feel
　　　very uncomfortable about their weight.
　　　我覺得當醫生告訴他們該減肥時，他們就要試著減肥，或是他們對體
　　　重感到不適的時候，也該要減肥。

老師：What do you think is the most important thing to do
　　　to lose weight？
　　　你覺得減肥最重要的事是什麼？

學生：I think the most important thing to do to lose weight
　　　is to have the self-discipline to exercise and eat right.
　　　我覺得減肥最重要的工作，就是自律地運動而且吃得恰當。

** ─────────────────

　　uncomfortable〔ʌnˋkʌmfətəbl̩〕*adj.* 不舒服的

◆ 標準體重計算表 ◆

性別	身高	標準體重	備註
男	170公分	62公斤	身高每增減 1 公分 體重增減 0.6 公斤
女	158公分	52公斤	身高每增減 1 公分 體重增減 0.5 公斤

此表摘自行政院衛生署國民營養指導手冊

註：為求計算方便，可採用下列方式來計算標準體重：
男：（身高－80）× 0.7
女：（身高－70）× 0.6

13. Sports 運動

📞 *打電話問老師問題*

1. What types of sports do you enjoy?
   你喜歡那種運動?

2. What sports do you actually have time to practice?
   你實際上有時間做什麼運動?

3. Would you say that you're a big sports fan?
   你是個狂熱的運動迷嗎?

4. Do you have a favorite sport?
   你有最喜歡的運動嗎?

5. Do you have a favorite sports athlete?
   你有最喜歡的運動員嗎?

6. What sports do you watch on TV?
   你觀賞電視上什麼運動?

7. How important do you think sports are to everyone?
   你覺得運動對每個人有多重要?

8. What is a good sport for someone to start with?
   若想做運動,應從什麼著手呢?

9. Do you think young people are getting enough exercise
   these days? 你覺得年輕人現在有足夠的運動量嗎?

10. Do you think any sports are too dangerous?
    你是否覺得什麼運動太危險?

📞 *打電話和老師討論問題*

Dialogue 1

老師： What types of sports do you enjoy?
你喜歡那種運動？

學生： I enjoy a fair range of sports, from basketball to tennis. But I don't get too much time these days to practice sports.
我喜歡的運動範圍相當廣泛，從籃球到網球都是。但我現在並沒有太多的時間做運動。

老師： What sports do you actually have time to practice, then?
那麼你實際上有時間做什麼運動？

學生： I play soccer, and I also go to the local high school playground with a few friends in the early morning. We *shoot* a few *hoops*.
我踢足球，並且也在清晨時，和幾個朋友到本地高中的運動場打籃球。

老師： Would you say that you're a big sports fan?
你是個狂熱的運動迷嗎？

學生： Not really. I watch a lot on TV, but I'm not the sports-addict type. I play sports for the fun of it rather than for good health, although I know it is good for me when I play ball.
不盡然。我看很多運動節目，但我並不是沈迷於運動那一型的。我運動是因為好玩，而不是為了健康，雖然我知道打球對我有益。

**

range (rendʒ) *n.* 範圍　　soccer ('sɑkɚ) *n.* 足球
playground ('ple‚graʊnd) *n.* 運動場　　hoops (hups) *n.* 籃球（俚）
fan (fæn) *n.* 迷　　addict ('ædɪkt) *n.* 上癮者；沈迷者

Dialogue 2

老師： Do you have a favorite sport ?
你有最喜歡的運動嗎？

學生： I suppose it would have to be soccer. It is because of the level of excitement you attain while playing. My favorite European team is Barcelona, and my favorite international team is Brazil.

應該是足球，我想是因為玩球時所能達到的興奮程度。我最喜歡的歐洲球隊是巴塞隆納，而最喜歡的國際球隊是巴西。

→ attain (ə'ten) v. 達到　Barcelona (,barsḷ'onə) n. 巴塞隆納

老師： Do you have a favorite sports athlete ?
你有最喜歡的運動員嗎？

學生： I think the only athlete who is truly ahead of his generation is Michael Jordan. He is a tremendously talented athlete, who has excelled in every way possible--He's a real inspiration for sports fans around the world.

我覺得唯一能超越當代的運動員是麥可・喬登。他是極具天分的運動員，在各方面都盡可能表現卓越——他給予全世界的運動迷莫大的鼓舞。

→ athlete ('æθlit) n. 運動員　tremendously (trɪ'mɛndəslɪ) adv. 非常
inspiration (,ɪnspə'reʃən) n. 給予鼓舞的人

老師： What sports do you watch on TV ?
你觀賞電視上什麼運動？

學生： I watch a lot of tennis, especially when Wimbledon is on. I think playing on a grass surface is the most challenging. My favorite player in the world at the moment is Pete Sampras.

我看很多網球，尤其是溫布頓開打的時候。我覺得在草皮上打球最具挑戰性。目前世界上我最喜歡的選手是皮特・山普拉斯。

→ Wimbledon ('wɪmbḷdən) n. 溫布頓

Dialogue 3

老師：How important do you think sports are to everyone?
你覺得運動對每個人有多重要?

學生：For the youth, it is a way of helping them grow stronger. For adults, it's a way of *maintaining their fitness*. For the old, it is a way to strengthen and prolong life through exercise.
對年輕人而言，那是幫助他們變得更強壯的方法。對成人而言，那是保持健康之道。對老年人而言，透過運動可使自己強壯，並延長壽命。
→ maintain ﹝ men'ten ﹞ v. 保持　　fitness ﹝'fɪtnɪs ﹞ n. 健康

老師：What is a good sport for someone to start with?
若想做運動，應從什麼著手呢?

學生：There are sports which *cater to* people of different ages, sizes and athletic abilities. Jogging is good for beginners because you can pace yourself; start with a short distance and then work your way upwards.
有各種運動能迎合不同年紀、體型和運動能力的人。慢跑對初學者很好，因為你能自己控制步調;你可以從短距離開始，然後慢慢推進增加。
→ cater ﹝'ketə﹞ v. 迎合　　pace ﹝ pes ﹞ v. 調整步調

老師：Do you think young people are getting enough exercise these days?
你覺得年輕人現在有足夠的運動嗎?

學生：I think they are content with what they have, but I would like to see more sports facilities such as ball courts, swimming pools and so on. Exercising is healthier than singing at the KTV!
我覺得他們對既有的感到很滿足，但我希望能看到更多的運動設施，像是球場、游泳池等等。運動比在 KTV 唱歌健康許多。
→ facilities ﹝ fə'sɪlətɪz ﹞ n. 設施　　court ﹝ kɔrt , kort ﹞ n. 球場

運動種類

badminton〔'bædmɪntən〕n. 羽毛球
baseball〔'bes,bɔl〕n. 棒球
basketball〔'bæskɪt,bɔl〕n. 籃球
billiards〔'bɪljədz〕n. 撞球
bowling〔'bolɪŋ〕n. 保齡球
boxing〔'baksɪŋ〕n. 拳擊
cricket〔'krɪkɪt〕n. 板球
diving〔'daɪvɪŋ〕n. 潛水
football〔'fut,bɔl〕n. 橄欖球
American football 美式足球
golf〔gɑlf, gɔlf〕n. 高爾夫
handball〔'hænd,bɔl〕n. 手球
hockey〔'hakɪ〕n. 曲棍球

ice hockey 冰上曲棍球
jogging〔'dʒagɪŋ〕n. 慢跑
judo〔'dʒudo〕n. 柔道
karate〔kə'rate〕n. 空手道
polo〔'polo〕n. 馬球
skating〔'sketɪŋ〕n. 溜冰
softball〔'sɔft,bɔl〕n. 壘球
table tennis 桌球
volleyball〔'valɪ,bɔl〕n. 排球
water polo 水球
track and field 田徑
weight-lifting 舉重
wrestling〔'rɛslɪŋ〕n. 摔角；相撲

球場類別

basketball court 籃球場
badminton court 羽球場
football field 橄欖球場
bowling alley 保齡球場
＊alley〔'ælɪ〕n. 巷道；球道
volleyball court 排球場
tennis court 網球場
billiards room 撞球場
cricket pitch 板球場

golf links 高爾夫球場
diving pool 跳水池
swimming pool 游泳池
mat〔mæt〕n. 拳擊台
baseball field 棒球場
soccer field 足球場
track〔træk〕n. 跑道
table〔'tebl̩〕n. 球檯

☆ 運動相關語彙

Olympic Games 國際奧林匹克運動會

open competition 公開賽　　　　invitation match 邀請賽

friendly competition 友誼賽

exhibition game 表演賽　＊exhibition〔،ɛksə'bɪʃən〕*n.* 表演

elimination game 淘汰賽　＊elimination〔ɪ،lɪmə'neʃən〕*n.* 淘汰

trial〔'traɪəl〕*n.* 預賽　　cycling race 循環賽

final 決賽　　　　　　semifinal〔،sɛmə'faɪnḷ〕*n.* 準決賽

crown fight 衛冕賽　＊crown〔kraʊn〕*n.* 榮冠

seeded team 種子隊　　home team 地主隊

amateur〔'æmə،tʃʊr〕*n.* 業餘選手

professional〔prə'fɛʃənḷ〕*n.* 職業選手

coach〔kotʃ〕*n.* 教練　　captain〔'kæptɪn〕*n.* 隊長

umpire〔'ʌmpaɪr〕*n.* 裁判

rooter 啦啦隊　＊root〔rut〕*v.* （美俚）鼓舞

default〔dɪ'fɔlt〕*n.* 棄權　　even 和局

decathlon〔dɪ'kæθlɑn〕*n.* 十項運動

torch〔tortʃ〕*n.* 聖火　　team work 團隊合作

cage ace 籃球名將　＊ace〔es〕*n.* 傑出人才

center 中鋒　　　　forward 前鋒

guard 後衛　　　　foul〔faʊl〕*n.* 犯規

interval〔'ɪntəvḷ〕*n.* 休息時間

smash〔smæʃ〕*n.* 殺球　　single game 單打

double game 雙打　　pitcher〔'pɪtʃə〕*n.* 投手

catcher 捕手　　　batter 打擊者

14. Family 家庭

📞 *打電話問老師問題*

1. Where does your family live? 你的家人住在那兒?

2. How many people are there in your family?
   你家有多少人?

3. Who do you include in your family?
   你的家庭包括那些成員?

4. Have you ever been to a family reunion?
   你參加過家庭聚會嗎?

5. Do you have a favorite family member?
   你有最喜歡的家人嗎?

6. What is special about your family?
   你的家庭有何特別之處?

7. What is your favorite family event?
   你最喜歡的家庭活動是什麼?

8. Is your family very close? 你的家人很親密嗎?

9. Did/do you have a special family pet?
   你家有養什麼特別的寵物嗎?

10. How often do you see your family?
    你多久和家人見一次面?

11. Do you have a favorite relative?
    你有最喜歡的親戚嗎?

📞 打電話和老師討論問題

Dialogue 1

老師：Where does your family live？ 你的家人住在那兒？

學生：Some members live in Taipei, some live in other parts of Taiwan, and I even have uncles that live in Canada. My family is *all over the world*！
有些住在台北，有些住台灣其他的地方。我甚至還有叔叔住在加拿大，我的家人遍及世界各地！

老師：That's a big family！ How many people are there in your family？ 眞是個大家庭！你家一共有多少人？

學生：There are around 30 members *in all*. It's an average sized family.
合計起來大約三十人，算是一般大小的家庭。
→ *in all* 合計

老師：Who do you include in your family？
你的家庭包括那些成員？

學生：I have included all my aunts and uncles from both of my parents' sides.
我把父母親兩邊的叔伯、姑姑、阿姨、舅舅都算進去了。

老師：Have you ever been to a family reunion？
你參加過家庭聚會嗎？

學生：Of course！ Every Chinese New Year we have a mass family reunion where all members of my family *get together for festive celebrations*.
當然！每逢農曆新年我們會有個大型的家庭聚會，所有的家庭成員會齊聚歡度節慶。
→ reunion〔rɪ'junjən〕*n.* 聚會　　festive〔'fɛstɪv〕*adj.* 節日的

Dialogue 2

老師： Do you have a favorite family member?
你有最喜歡的家人嗎?

學生： Naturally I love all members of my family, but I have
to say that I do tend to favor my younger sister.
所有的家人我當然都愛,但我必須說,我的確比較喜歡我妹妹。

老師： What is special about your family?
你的家庭有何特別之處嗎?

學生： I think the special thing about my family is that we
are all over the world. I have relatives in North America, Europe and even Australia. But then again in Taiwan these days a lot of people are moving abroad......
我想最特別的是我們散布在世界各地。我有親戚在北美、歐洲,甚
至澳洲。不過話又說回來,台灣現在有許多人都在移民……

老師： What is your favorite "family" event?
你最喜歡的家庭活動是什麼?

學生： I suppose it would have to be the annual reunion at
Chinese New Year. I love it for two reasons: One, I
get to see all my cousins and two, I get a lot of
money from the red envelopes!
我想是一年一度的春節團圓,我喜歡的原因有二:一是我可以見到
所有的堂兄妹、表姊弟,二是我可以收到很多紅包錢。

** ————————————

favor〔'fevɚ〕v. 偏愛   annual〔'ænjʊəl〕adj. 一年一度的
cousin〔'kʌzn̩〕n. 堂兄弟;表姊妹
red envelope 紅包

Dialogue 3

老師： Is your family very close?
你的家人很親密嗎？

學生： I think we are. Or at least, the relatives in Taiwan are close. We visit each other often and we eat together on weekends. For example, all the members of my family who live in Taipei get together for a meal during weekends.
我想是的，至少在台灣的家人是如此。我們經常拜訪彼此，在週末一起聚餐。像我在台北的家人就會在週末的時候，聚在一起吃頓飯。

老師： Did/do you have a special family pet?
你家有養什麼特別的寵物嗎？

學生： I had a special pet. It was a dog called Pipi. I had raised it from the day it was adopted. Every time I see a photo of it childhood memories *run though my head*! Pipi lived until 14, which is quite old for a dog.
我養過一隻特別的寵物，是隻叫皮皮的小狗。從它被收養的那天起，我就一直照顧它。每當我看著它的照片，童年的回憶便浮現在我的腦海裡。皮皮活了十四歲，對狗來說算相當長壽。

老師： How often do you see your family?
你多久和家人見一次面？

學生： Well, I see most of my relatives in Taipei almost on a weekly basis, but I don't get to see family members who live abroad very often.
我和台北的親戚大約每星期見面一次，但和旅居國外的親人難得見面。

**
adopt (ə'dɑpt) v. 收養

15. Friendship 友 情

📞 *打電話問老師問題*

1. Do you have a best friend? 你有最要好的朋友嗎？

2. Do you have a large circle of friends?
   你的交遊廣闊嗎？

3. How did you meet most of your friends?
   你和大部分的朋友是如何認識的？

4. What do you think makes someone a good friend?
   你覺得什麼樣的人才算是好朋友？

5. Do you think you are a good friend?
   你認為自己是個好朋友嗎？

6. Are you loyal to your friends? 你對朋友忠實嗎？

7. What do you like to do with your friends?
   你喜歡和朋友做些什麼事？

8. Do you spend a lot of time with your friends?
   你花很多時間和朋友相處嗎？

9. How important are your friendships to you?
   友情對你有多重要？

10. What do you talk about with your friends?
    你和朋友都談論什麼？

11. Are all of your friends about your same age?
    你的朋友和你的年紀相仿嗎？

打電話和老師討論問題

Dialogue 1

老師：Do you have a best friend?
你有最要好的朋友嗎？

學生：Yes. She is like a sister to me. I have known her since we were in elementary school.
有，她就像我的姊妹。我們從小學起就認識了。

老師：Do you have a *large circle of friends*?
你的交遊廣闊嗎？

學生：I don't have too many friends because I am too shy. Instead, I have a small circle of very close friends.
我沒有太多朋友，因爲我太害羞了。不過，我有一些非常要好的朋友。

老師：How did you meet most of your friends?
你和大部分的朋友是如何認識的？

學生：I met most of my friends when I was a university student. Some of my friends lived in the same dormitory as I did, and others studied the same major as I did.
我和大部分的朋友是在大學時認識的。有些朋友和我住在同一棟宿舍，有些則是同科系的同學。

** ——————————

elementary (ˌɛləˈmɛntərɪ) *adj.* 初級的
dormitory (ˈdɔrməˌtorɪ) *n.* 宿舍
major (ˈmedʒɚ) *n.* 主修課程

Dialogue 2

老師： What do you think makes someone a good friend ?
你覺得什麼樣的人才算是好朋友？

學生： I think a good friend is supportive to his or her friends. Also, I think a good friend is willing to help his or her friends when they are in trouble.
我認為好朋友會支持自己的朋友。此外，好朋友也樂意幫助患難中的朋友。

老師： Do you think you are a good friend ?
你認為自己是個好的朋友嗎？

學生： I hope so. I try to help my friends in every way I can.
希望是。我竭盡所能來幫助自己的朋友。

老師： Are you loyal to your friends ?　你對朋友忠實嗎？

學生： Yes, I think I'm a very loyal person. I never *reveal any secrets* my friends tell me, so they love to talk to me.
是的，我想我是個相當忠心的人。我從不洩露朋友告訴我的祕密，所以他們都喜歡和我談心。
→ loyal (ˈlɔɪəl , ˈlɔjəl) *adj.* 忠實的

Dialogue 3

老師： What do you like to do with your friends ?
你喜歡和朋友做些什麼事？

學生： I like to go out to eat, watch movies, and go shopping with my friends. Sometimes we gather at a friend's house, talking all night long.
我喜歡和朋友出去吃飯、看電影、逛街。有時我們會聚在某個朋友的家裡，聊一整個晚上的天。

老師 : Do you spend a lot of time with your friends?
你花很多時間和朋友相處嗎?

學生 : I don't spend too much time with my friends because we are all very busy. But, we spend a lot of time talking on the telephone.
我沒有花太多的時間和朋友在一起,因為我們都太忙了。不過我們花很多時間講電話。

老師 : How important are your friendships to you?
友情對你有多重要?

學生 : My friendships are very important to me because they are like family to me. They are the best listeners when I need *a shoulder to cry on*.
友情對我來說很重要,因為朋友就像家人一樣。當我需要訴苦時,他們是最佳的聽眾。

** ────────

cry on one's shoulder 向某人訴苦

A friend in need is a friend indeed.

── 患難見真情

16. Divorce 離 婚

📞 *打電話問老師問題*

1. Do you approve of divorce？ 你贊成離婚嗎？

2. Have any of the marriages in your family ended in divorce？ 你的家人之中，有沒有人的婚姻以離婚收場？

3. Would you ever have a divorce？ 你會離婚嗎？

4. Do you believe mothers should receive custody of their children？ 你認爲母親應該獲得監護權嗎？

5. Do you think the spouse without custody of the children should pay child support？
你認爲沒有監護權的配偶應該付子女扶養費嗎？

6. Do you think the wealthier spouse should pay alimony after the divorce？
你認爲經濟情況較好的配偶，離婚之後應該付贍養費嗎？

7. Do you think there are too many divorces？
你認爲離婚案件太多了嗎？

8. When do you believe divorce is most harmful？
你認爲離婚在什麼情況下最具傷害力？

9. When do you believe divorce is beneficial？
你認爲在什麼情況下，離婚是有利的？

10. When do you think couples should get divorced？
什麼時候你覺得夫妻應該離婚？

📞 *打電話和老師討論問題*

Dialogue 1

老師： Do you approve of divorce?
你贊成離婚嗎?

學生： I neither approve nor disapprove of divorce. I think divorce is an unfortunate necessity for some couples.
我不贊成也不反對離婚。我認為離婚對一些夫妻而言,是件不幸但必然的事。

老師： Have any of the marriages in your family ended in divorce?
你的家人之中,有沒有人的婚姻以離婚收場?

學生： Yes, one of my aunts got divorced after being married for only one year.
有,我一位姑姑結婚才一年就離婚了。

老師： Would you ever have a divorce?
你會離婚嗎?

學生： I hope not. But, if my spouse were abusive, I would have to get a divorce rather than tolerate the violence.
我希望不會。不過,如果我的配偶有暴力行為,我會離婚而不會選擇忍受暴力。

** _____

approve〔ə'pruv〕v. 贊成　　　divorce〔də'vors〕n. v. 離婚
necessity〔nə'sɛsətɪ〕n. 必要　　spouse〔spauz〕n. 配偶
abusive〔ə'bjusɪv〕adj. 虐待的

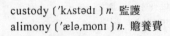

Dialogue 2

老師： Do you believe mothers should receive custody of their children ?
你認為母親應該獲得孩子的監護權嗎？

學生： I think the parent with whom the child is closest should receive custody. Usually, children are closer to their mothers.
我認為和孩子較親的一方應該獲得監護權。通常，孩子都比較親近母親。

老師： Do you think the spouse without custody of the children should pay child support ?
你認為沒有監護權的配偶應該付子女扶養費嗎？

學生： Certainly. I believe parents should be responsible for their children, even if they don't have custody of them.
當然。我相信父母對自己的子女有責任，即使他們沒有監護權。

老師： Do you think the wealthier spouse should pay alimony after the divorce ?
你認為經濟情況較好的配偶，離婚之後應該付贍養費嗎？

學生： I think the wealthier spouse should pay alimony only if the other spouse really needs financial support.
我認為只有在另一配偶真正需要金錢援助時，經濟情況較好的一方才需付贍養費。

** ————————————

custody ('kʌstədɪ) *n.* 監護
alimony ('ælə,monɪ) *n.* 贍養費

Dialogue 3

老師：Do you think there are too many divorces?
你認為離婚案件太多了嗎？

學生：Yes. I think couples should try harder to stay together. They should get to know each other better before they get married.
是的，我認為夫妻應該努力維持婚姻。他們應該在結婚以前就深入認識彼此。

老師：When do you believe divorce is most harmful?
你認為離婚在什麼情況下最具傷害力？

學生：I believe divorce is most harmful when there are small children involved. Children become very confused and upset when their parents get divorced. A large number of *juvenile delinquents* come from broken families.
我認為當有幼兒牽連其中時，離婚是最具傷害力的。當父母離婚時，孩子會覺得迷惑、變得不安。許多不良少年、少女都是來自破碎的家庭。

老師：When do you believe divorce is beneficial?
你認為在什麼情況下離婚是有利的？

學生：I believe divorce is beneficial if the marriage is very destructive. If the spouses are seriously hurting one another, then it is better for them to be apart.
我相信如果婚姻具毀滅性，離婚便是有利的。如果配偶嚴重傷害對方，分手對他們來說較好。

** ————————

involve (ɪn'vɑlv) v. 牽連　　juvenile ('dʒuvə,naɪl) adj. 少年的
delinquent (dɪ'lɪŋkwənt) n. 行為不良者
destructive (dɪ'strʌktɪv) adj. 毀滅的

17. Moving 搬 家

📞 *打電話問老師問題*

1. What does it cost to move in your country?
   在你們國家，搬家有那些開銷？

2. Why did you make your last move?
   你上次為什麼搬家？

3. How many times have you moved?
   你搬過幾次家？

4. What do you like most about moving?
   搬家有那方面是你最喜歡的？

5. What kind of problems did you have moving?
   你搬家有遇到什麼問題嗎？

6. Did you ever have any big moves?
   你有過大搬家嗎？

7. Did you move out of your home when you went to college?
   你上大學時，搬到外頭住嗎？

8. Is it expensive to move in Taiwan?
   在台灣搬家會不會很貴？

9. Why is it difficult to move in Taiwan?
   為什麼搬家在台灣來說不容易？

📞 *打電話和老師討論問題*

Dialogue 1

老師： What does it cost to move in Taiwan?
在台灣，搬家有那些開銷？

學生： You have to hire moving vans and probably people to help you move the furniture, and *sort out* the details with the telephone, gas, water and electric companies.
你得雇用搬運貨車，甚或請人來幫你搬傢俱。你還得和電話、瓦斯、自來水以及電力公司解決細節。

老師： Why did you make your last move?
你上次爲什麼搬家？

學生： I was renting a house and I decided that it was time for me to have a place of my own.
我以前都是租房子，不過我覺得是該有一個屬於自己的地方了。

老師： How many times have you moved?
你搬過家幾次？

學生： Altogether, four times. I don't really like to move because there's too much hassle involved, and I don't like to waste time moving. I prefer to spend my time on other more important things.
一共四次。我不太喜歡搬家，因爲老是有許多麻煩，而且我也不喜歡浪費時間去搬家。我寧願把時間花在其他較重要的事情上。

＊＊

sort sth out 整理好；解決　　furniture (ˈfɝnɪtʃɚ) *n.* 傢俱
van (væn) *n.* 貨車　　hire (haɪr) *v.* 雇用
hassle (ˈhæsl̩) *n.* 困難；掙扎　　involve (ɪnˈvɑlv) *v.* 涉入

Dialogue 2

老師： What do you like most about moving?
搬家有那方面是你最喜歡的?

學生： There's not a lot I like about moving, but I suppose meeting new people and making new friends can be an enjoyable experience.
搬家沒有什麼讓我喜歡的,但是我認為看看新面孔、交些新朋友也是令人愉快的經驗。

老師： What kind of problems did you have moving?
你搬家有遇到什麼問題嗎?

學生： I had a lot of furniture to move around and I moved on a rainy day, so some of my furniture got wet. It was an unforgettable experience, but a bad one.
我有很多的傢俱要搬,而搬家的那天是個下雨天,所以我的一些傢俱都淋溼了。那是個難忘但卻不愉快的經驗。

老師： Did you ever have any big moves?
你有過大搬家嗎?

學生： Once I had to help a friend move. His new house was so big that it took a whole week to move everything. It was in Taiwan, so it was expensive, too.
有一次,我得幫一個朋友搬家。他的新家很大,所以我們整整花了一星期的時間,搬完所有的東西。因為是在台灣,所以也很貴。

** ————————————

enjoyable〔 ɪn'dʒɔɪəbl̩ 〕 *adj.* 令人快樂的
unforgettable〔 ˌʌnfɚ'gɛtəbl̩ 〕 *adj.* 不能忘記的

Dialogue 3

老師：Did you move out of your home when you went to college?

你上大學時搬到外頭住嗎？

學生：Yes. My family is in Taipei, but my school is located in Kaohsiung. I moved a lot when I was a student in college. I moved every year from house to house, living with classmates.

是的。我家在台北，但是學校位在高雄。我在大學時常搬家，我每年都換房子，和同學一起合租。

老師：Is it expensive to move in Taiwan?

在台灣搬家會不會很貴？

學生：It can be. If you don't plan everything out, you will probably *end up* spending a lot more than you should. Moving the smaller furniture by yourself rather than hiring companies saves you money, for example.

會哦！如果你沒有籌畫好一切，最後可能會多花很多不必要的錢。比方說，較小的傢俱你自己搬而不要請公司，就可以省錢。

老師：Why is it difficult to move in Taiwan?

為什麼搬家在台灣來說不容易？

學生：Because the roads in Taiwan are always so full, and space is limited in the cities. It is hard to move large pieces of furniture around.

在台灣因為道路總是擁塞，而都市裡的空間也有限制，所以大傢俱的搬運很困難。

** ————————————

locate〔lo'ket〕v. 位於　　*plan* (*out*) 策畫；籌畫

18. Emigration 移 民

📞 *打電話問老師問題*

1. Do people in your country emigrate to foreign countries ?
   貴國有人移居他國嗎？

2. Why do people move away from your country ?
   為什麼人民要搬離你們的國家？

3. Where do people in your country emigrate to ?
   貴國的人民移民到那裡？

4. Do you know anyone who has emigrated to another country ?
   你認識的人中，有人移民到國外嗎？

5. Are you still in touch with your friends who have emigrated ?
   你仍和移民的朋友保持聯繫嗎？

6. How do your friends find life in another country ?
   你的朋友認為國外的生活如何？

7. Are there foreign immigrants in your country ?
   有外國人移民到你的國家嗎？

8. Do you know any foreign immigrants ?
   你認識任何國外來的居民嗎？

9. Would you ever emigrate to another country ?
   你會移民到他國嗎？

📞 打電話和老師討論問題

Dialogue 1

老師： Do people in Taiwan emigrate to foreign countries?
台灣的人移民到國外嗎?

學生： They do. And the number of people emigrating is *on the increase*, too. More and more people are moving out of Taiwan every year.
是的，而且移民的人數還在增加中。每年有愈來愈多的人移出台灣。

老師： Why do people move away from Taiwan?
為什麼民眾要搬離台灣?

學生： In the past it was for the fear of attack from mainland China. Nowadays some people feel that the education in Taiwan is too demanding for their kids; some are simply *fed up with* the level of pollution in the cities.
在以前是因為懼怕中共犯台。現在有些人認為，台灣的教育對兒童而言過於嚴厲；有些則是受夠都市的污染。

老師： Where do people in Taiwan emigrate to?
台灣的人移民到那裡?

學生： Most people used to emigrate to the States. Now there is an increasing number of people who emigrate to Canada, Australia, New Zealand and England. A lot of parents send their kids to the States or the UK for education.
以往大部分的人移民到美國，現在則有愈來愈多的人移民到加拿大、澳洲、紐西蘭和英國。很多父母將小孩送到美國或英國受教育。

**

emigrate〔ˋɛməˌgret〕v. 移居他國　　attack〔əˋtæk〕n. 攻擊
demanding〔dɪˋmændɪŋ〕adj. 嚴厲的　　*be fed up with* 厭煩

Dialogue 2

老師： Do you know anyone who has emigrated to another country ?

你認識的人中，有人移民到國外嗎？

學生： One of my uncles went to study for an MBA in the States. After graduation he stayed there, and now he has a family. Quite a few of my former classmates have also emigrated to the States and Canada.

我一個叔叔到美國去攻讀企管碩士學位。畢業後，他留在那裡，並且成家立業。我有不少以前的同學也都移民到美國和加拿大。

老師： Are you still in touch with your friends who have emigrated ?

你仍和移民的朋友保持聯繫嗎？

學生： Yes. We used to write letters and recently we have been *keeping in touch* with e-mail and IRC.

是的，我們曾經通過信，而最近我們改以電子郵件和線上交談來保持聯繫。

They all miss Taiwan very much, and most of them come back here in the summer to see their relatives and in some cases, parents.

他們都很想念台灣，大部分的人會在夏天的時候回到這兒，探望親戚或是父母。

**

MBA 企管碩士（ = *Master of Business Administration*）
IRC 線上交談（ = *Internet Relay Chat*）

老師：How do your friends find life in another country？

你的朋友認為國外的生活如何？

學生：They have adjusted to life abroad well and are *getting along* just fine with the locals, nevertheless they miss Taiwan. They still miss the night markets, the busy streets, and the thriving nightlife of Taiwan.

他們對國外的生活已經適應良好，並且和當地居民相處融洽，然而他們還是想念台灣。他們想念夜市、忙碌的街道，以及繁華的台灣夜生活。

→ adjust〔ə'dʒʌst〕*v.* 適應　　*get along* 相處
local〔lokl〕*n.* 當地居民　　thriving〔'θraɪvɪŋ〕*adj.* 繁榮的

Dialogue 3

老師：Are there foreign immigrants in Taiwan？

台灣有外國來的居民嗎？

學生：Yes. Some are sent here from foreign companies, and some are here to serve as workers or English teachers. Once their time is up, some of them choose to stay here because they like it so much. They are popular with a lot of locals.

有。有些是國外公司派來此地，有些來這兒做工或教英文。一旦他們的滯留期到了，有部分會選擇待在這裡，因為他們深愛此地。他們受到許多居民的歡迎。

老師：Would you ever emigrate to another country？

你會移民到他國嗎？

學生：I don't think so. *After all*, Taiwan is my home and all my family and friends are here. Instead of *leaving the problem behind*, I think we should all work to solve the problems we have such as pollution and education！

我不認為。畢竟台灣是我的家鄉，我的家人與朋友都在這兒。我覺得與其將問題拋諸腦後，還不如大家努力來解決污染和教育等問題。

老師：Do you know any foreign immigrants？
你認識任何從國外來的居民嗎？

學生：Actually I do. I was in a pub one weekend with a few friends, and I met an American, who was here teaching English. We go out sometimes and do a language exchange: I help him with Mandarin, and he helps me out with my English.
我的確認識。有個週末我和一些朋友到一間酒吧，在那兒我認識了一位來此地教英文的美國人。我們有時一起出去玩，還做了語言交換：我教他國語，而他教我英文。

心得筆記欄

19. Learning Languages
學習語言

打電話問老師問題

1. How many languages can you speak?
   你會幾種語言？

2. Can you speak these languages fluently?
   這幾種語言你可以講得很流利嗎？

3. Why did you study these languages?
   你為什麼會學這些語言？

4. What's the most difficult language you've studied?
   你學過最難的語言是什麼？

5. What's the easiest language you've studied?
   你學過最簡單的語言是什麼？

6. What do you think is the most difficult part of learning a language?
   你認為學語言時，最困難的部分是什麼？

7. Do you have any strategies in learning languages?
   你在學習語言方面有什麼策略嗎？

8. What do you think is the best way to learn a language?
   你覺得學習語言最好的方式是什麼？

9. Have you ever had to use the language skills that you've learned? 你曾經遇到過必須使用所學語言技巧的情況嗎？

📞 *打電話和老師討論問題*

Dialogue 1

老師： How many languages can you speak?
你會幾種語言？

學生： I can speak three languages: Taiwanese, which is my *mother tongue*, Mandarin, because it's the official language, and English, which is what I learn at school.
我會三種語言：台語，那是我的母語；國語，因為那是官方語言，以及我在學校學的英語。

老師： Can you speak these languages fluently?
這幾種語言你可以講得很流利嗎？

學生： Of course I can speak Mandarin and Taiwanese fluently. As for English, I know enough to get around, but I am still a bit nervous when it comes to conversation.
國語和台語我當然可以說得很流利，至於英語，溝通上是夠用，但是該開口的時候，我還是會有點緊張。

老師： Why did you study these languages?
你為什麼會學這些語言？

學生： Every student in Taiwan has to study English. Actually I like it quite a bit. I think it's mainly because of the teacher. He's a really good teacher, and he makes you want to know more.
台灣的學生都必須學英語。事實上我相當喜歡它，我想主要的原因是老師的關係。他真的是位好老師，引發你的求知慾。

**

---

tongue〔tʌŋ〕*n.* 語言　　Mandarin〔'mændərɪn〕*n.* 國語
fluently〔'fluəntlɪ〕*adv.* 流利地

Dialogue 2

老師： What's the most difficult language you've studied？
你學過最難的語言是什麼？

學生： I think that would have to be French. I gave up after six months because there were so many different tenses. Also I think my teacher wasn't committed enough to stimulate my interest in French.
我想應該是法語。我學了六個月就放棄，因為它的時態實在太多。此外，我認為老師教學不夠認真，所以無法引起我對法語的興趣。

老師： What's the easiest language you've studied？
你學過最簡單的語言是什麼？

學生： English. I like it so I spend more time than the average student learning it; also there is plenty of educational material available to further my ability. I also watch a lot of movies to improve my comprehension.
英語。我喜歡它，所以我比一般學生多花功夫去學習。此外，有許多的教材可供我提昇我的能力。我還看了許多電影來加強我的理解力。

老師： What do you think is the most difficult part of learning a language？
你認為學語言時，最困難的部分是什麼？

學生： I think it's ***getting used to*** the grammar and also finding the time to practice it. I think the most important part of learning any language is practice.
我認為是熟習文法，以及找時間來練習。我認為學任何語言，最重要的部分就是練習。

**────────────

tense〔tɛns〕*n.* 時態　　commit〔kə'mɪt〕*v.* 投入
stimulate〔'stɪmjə,let〕*v.* 刺激；鼓舞　　available〔ə'veləbl〕*adj.* 可得到的
comprehension〔,kɑmprɪ'hɛnʃən〕*n.* 理解力

Dialogue 3

老師：Do you have any strategies in learning languages?
你在學習語言方面有什麼策略嗎?

學生：Well, I try to memorize a few new words every day. In order to be good at a language you must be interested in it. Since I'm interested in learning English, I do not find studying it a hassle.
我試著每天背一些新單字。為了專精某種語言，你必須對它感興趣。由於我對學英語感興趣，所以我不覺得讀起來有什麼困難。

老師：What do you think is the best way to learn a language?
你覺得學習語言最好的方式是什麼?

學生：I try to practice **by all means** possible. As I've said, I watch movies, and I have a pen pal in Canada, too. I practice English every day because I think being consistent is very important.
我試著以各種方法來練習。正如我所說的，我看電影，而且我還有個加拿大筆友。我每天練習英語，因為我認為恒心十分重要。

老師：Have you ever had to use the language skills that you have learned?
你曾經遇到過必須使用所學語言技巧的情況嗎?

學生：Once I was waiting for a bus when I saw a foreign tourist, who appeared to be lost. I managed to help her find her destination, and now we're pen pals.
有次我在等公車的時候，看見一位似乎迷路的觀光客。我幫她找到她的目的地，而我們現在成了筆友。

** ───────────────

strategy ('strætədʒɪ) *n.* 策略　　hassle ('hæsḷ) *n.* 奮戰
consistent (kən'sɪstənt) *adj.* 一致的；不變的
destination (,dɛstə'neʃən) *n.* 目的地

語言類別

Arabic〔'ærəbɪk〕阿拉伯語
Chinese〔tʃaɪ'niz〕中文
Danish〔'denɪʃ〕丹麥語
Esperanto〔͵ɛspə'rɑnto , -rænto〕世界語
French〔frɛntʃ〕法語
Hakkanese〔͵hɑkɑ'niz〕客家語
Hindi〔'hɪndi〕印度語
Indonesian〔͵ɪndə'niʃən , -ʒən〕印尼語
Italian〔ɪ'tæljən〕義大利語
Korean〔ko'riən〕韓語
Malay〔mə'le , 'me͵le〕馬來語
Norwegian〔nɔr'widʒən〕挪威語
Portuguese〔'portʃə͵giz〕葡萄牙語
Russian〔'rʌʃən〕俄語
Swedish〔'swidɪʃ〕瑞典語
Turkish〔'tɝkɪʃ〕土耳其語
Vietnamese〔vɪ͵ɛtnə'miz〕越南語
dialect〔'daɪəlɛkt〕*n.* 方言
linguistics〔lɪŋ'gwɪstɪks〕*n.* 語言學
accent〔'æksɛnt〕*n.* 口音
pidgin〔'pɪdʒɪn〕*n.* 不純正的語言
pidgin English 洋涇濱英語

Cantonese〔'kæntən'iz〕粵語
Czech〔tʃɛk〕捷克語
English〔'ɪŋglɪʃ〕英語

German〔'dʒɝmən〕德語
Hebrew〔'hibru〕希伯來語

Japanese〔͵dʒæpə'niz〕日本語
Latin〔'lætɪn〕拉丁語
Mandarin〔'mændərɪn〕國語

Spanish〔'spænɪʃ〕西班牙語
Thai〔taɪ〕泰語

Chinese

20. Studying Overseas
海外留學

📞 *打電話問老師問題*

1. Are there a lot of students from your country studying overseas？ 你們國家有許多學生出國留學嗎？

2. Why do students travel all the way to a foreign country to study？ 爲何學生要大老遠地到他國求學？

3. Are there any differences between the students who study overseas now and a few years ago？
   現在到海外的留學生和以前有什麼不同？

4. Do you have any friends who study overseas？
   你有沒有朋友出國留學？

5. Why would parents let their children go abroad to study by themselves？
   爲什麼父母會讓小孩單獨在國外念書？

6. What kind of problems do you think these students will face？ 你認爲這些學生會面臨什麼問題？

7. Do you think that the parents have to bear some responsibility？ 你覺得父母必須承擔一些責任嗎？

8. Do you think studying overseas is a good thing？
   你覺得出國留學好嗎？

9. Would you go abroad if you had the choice？
   如果你可以選擇，你會出國嗎？

📞 *打電話和老師討論問題*

Dialogue 1

老師： Are there a lot of students from Taiwan studying overseas ?

台灣有許多學生出國留學嗎？

學生： Yes. There has always been quite a number of students going overseas to pursue their studies, and in recent years the number of students going overseas is on the increase.

是的，一直都有不少學生出國求學，而最近幾年來，到海外留學的學生數目持續在增加。

老師： Why do students travel all the way to a foreign country to study ?

為何學生要大老遠地到他國求學？

學生： Some people believe that the quality of education overseas is higher than that in Taiwan.

有些人認為國外的教育品質比台灣高。

Also there are parents who are worried that their kids will do badly in Taiwan because of the pressure students are under.

也有些父母認為，在台灣的教育壓力下，他們的孩子留在台灣不會有所表現。

**

pursue〔pə'su , -'sɪu〕*v.* 追求　　quality〔'kwɑlətɪ〕*n.* 品質

老師： Are there any differences between the students who study overseas now and a few years ago?
現在到海外的台灣留學生和以前有什麼不同嗎？

學生： It used to be the case that most of the overseas students were students who had already completed university and were *in pursuit of* a Master's degree. Nowadays there are a lot of younger students traveling overseas to study.
在以往，大部分的海外留學生都是大學畢業後，才到國外攻讀碩士學位。現在則有很多年紀更小的學生，遠赴海外求學。
➡ pursuit (pə'sut , -'sjut) *n.* 追求；從事

Dialogue 2

老師： Do you have any friends who study overseas?
你有沒有朋友出國留學？

學生： I have a few classmates who went off to America and Europe to study. Some were only fifteen when they left Taiwan, and some of them are there by themselves. Their parents are still in Taiwan working.
我有一些同學去美國和歐洲念書。有些十五歲時就離開台灣，有些是單獨在外國，而父母仍留在台灣工作。

老師： Why would parents let their children go abroad to study by themselves?
為什麼父母會讓小孩單獨在國外念書？

學生： *As I have mentioned earlier*, some parents believe that the standard of education in foreign countries is better. Therefore they are sending their kids abroad in hope that their children will receive a better education.
正如我之前提到的，有些父母相信國外的教育水準較高，所以他們將孩子送往國外，希望他們能受到更好的教育。

老師： What kind of problems do you think these students will face? 你認爲這些學生會面臨什麼問題？

學生： I have a friend who is actually behaving worse than he was in Taiwan. He used to do quite well here, but when he went abroad, he felt isolated because he could not speak English very well, and his parents weren't there to guide him.

我有個朋友的行爲舉止，變得比在台灣時還糟。他在這兒本來表現良好，但是出國之後由於英文不好，便覺得受到孤立。而他的父母不在身旁，也無法督導他。

Dialogue 3

老師： Do you think that the parents have to bear some responsibility? 你覺得父母必須承擔一些責任嗎？

學生： I think so. A lot of the kids don't actually want to go overseas, but their parents force them to.

我是這麼認爲。有許多小孩並不想到國外，但是父母強迫他們去。

老師： Parents force their children to go abroad? I can't believe it!

父母逼小孩到國外去？我眞不敢相信。

學生： The parents feel that they're *doing the right thing*. They think they do it out of love, but I think the parents should think more about the feelings of their children if they really care about them.

父母親認爲他們的做法是對的。他們這麼做是出於愛，不過我認爲，如果父母眞的關心孩子，他們應該多考慮孩子的感受。

** ─────────

isolate (ˈaɪsḷˌet) v. 孤立

老師：Do you think studying overseas is a good thing?
你覺得出國留學好嗎？

學生：I think it is a good thing, but it isn't for everyone.
Some students are able to cope and excel, others are
not. Unless you plan everything out and think about
it carefully, you will undoubtedly regret it!
我認為是好事，但不是每個人都適合。有些學生禁得起競爭且出類
拔萃，但有些就是不行。除非你計畫周詳並且審慎考慮，否則你絕
對會後悔。

老師：Would you go abroad if you had the choice?
如果你可以選擇，你會出國嗎？

學生：I don't think I would right now because I am still in
high school, and I don't think the time is right. I
think I will go to another country, but only after I
graduate from college. I'm going to need more time
to get ready!
我不認為我會馬上去，因為我還是高中生，而且我覺得時機不對。
我想我會到別的國家，不過要等我大學畢業後。我需要更多的時間
來準備。

**

cope (kop) v. 競爭　　regret (rɪ'grɛt) v. 後悔

21. Occupation 工 作

📞 *打電話問老師問題*

1. When was the last time you performed a job hunt?
   你上回找工作是什麼時候?

2. How did you go about searching for a job?
   你如何著手找工作?

3. How long did it take you to find a job?
   你花了多久時間才找到工作?

4. Do you get nervous before job interviews?
   應徵面試時你會緊張嗎?

5. What do you do to prepare for a job interview?
   你如何準備應徵面試?

6. Do you think it is important to have a professional-looking résumé?
   你認為準備一份專業的履歷表很重要嗎?

7. Would you prefer to have one full-time job or two part-time jobs?
   你喜歡有一份全職的工作或是兩份兼職的工作?

8. Which is more important to you: money or job satisfaction?
   金錢或工作滿意度,那個對你較重要?

9. What would be your ideal occupation?
   你理想的職業是什麼?

📞 *打電話和老師討論問題*

Dialogue 1

老師： When was the last time you performed a job hunt?
你上回找工作是什麼時候？

學生： Two years ago, after I graduated from college.
兩年前，在我大學畢業之後。

老師： How did you go about searching for a job?
你如何著手找工作？

學生： I told my father's friends that I was looking for a job,
I answered classified advertisements, and I wrote letters
to companies that interested me.
我告訴父親的朋友我正在找工作，我回了求才廣告，我也寫信到我感
興趣的公司去。
➔ *go about* 著手

老師： How long did it take you to find a job?
你花了多久時間才找到工作？

學生： It took me almost two months to find my job.
我花了將近兩個月的時間才找到工作。

Dialogue 2

老師： What do you do to prepare for a job interview?
你如何準備應徵面試？

學生： I try to learn as much as possible about the company
that is interviewing me. I also review my strengths and
accomplishments.
我會盡量瞭解所要前往面試的公司，我也溫習自己的實力和技能。
➔ interview ('ɪntɚˌvju) *n. v.* 面談　　strength (strɛnθ) *n.* 實力
accomplishment (ə'kamplɪʃmənt) *n.* 技能；才藝

老師： Do you get nervous before job interviews?
應徵面試時你會緊張嗎?

學生： Of course. I think job interviews are very stressful. When I was waiting for my last interview, I couldn't sit still.
當然。我覺得應徵面試充滿了壓力。上回我在等面試的時候,就坐立難安。

老師： Do you think it is important to have a professional-looking résumé?　你認為準備一份專業的履歷表很重要嗎?

學生： Certainly. A good résumé highlights your strengths and impresses your interviewer.
當然。一份好的履歷表可以突顯你的實力,並且加深主考官的印象。
→ résumé (ˌrɛzu'me) *n.* 履歷表　　highlight ('haɪˌlaɪt) *v.* 使顯著

Dialogue 3

老師： Would you prefer to have one full-time job or two part-time jobs?
你喜歡有一份全職的工作,或是兩份兼差的工作?

學生： I would prefer to have one full-time job, so I would not have to commute between jobs.
我較喜歡一份全職的工作,這樣我才不必通勤往返各個工作。
→ commute (kə'mjut) *v.* 通勤

老師： Which is more important to you: money or job satisfaction?　金錢或工作滿意度,那個對你較重要?

學生： Both are important to me. It is difficult to be happy in your job without both money and job satisfaction.
兩者對我都很重要。金錢和工作滿意度不能兼顧的話,工作要愉快是很難的。

老師： What would be your ideal occupation？
你理想的職業是什麼？

學生： My ideal occupation would pay me a lot of money for doing something I love to do. But I guess it's not easy for me to find such an occupation.
我理想的職業是薪水多且做我喜歡的事。但是，我猜這種工作不好找。

☆ 工作相關語彙

job hunter 求職者

job-hopper 經常換工作的人　　＊hopper（'hɑpɚ）n. 跳躍物

moonlighter（'mun,laɪtɚ）n. 兼差者

employee（,ɛmplɔɪ'i , ɪm'plɔɪi）n. 職員

employer（ ɪm'plɔɪɚ）n. 雇主　　　casual laborer 臨時工

personnel cut 人事裁員　　　　　resign（rɪ'zaɪn）v. 辭職

retire（rɪ'taɪr）v. 退休　　　　　annuity（ə'njuətɪ）n. 養老金

wage（wedʒ）n. 工資　　　　　　strike（straɪk）n. 罷工

retiring allowance 退休金　　＊allowance（ə'lauəns）n. 津貼

depression（dɪ'prɛʃən）n. 不景氣

unemployed（,ʌnɪm'plɔɪd）adj. 失業的

severance pay 遣散費　　＊severance（'sɛvərəns）n. 斷絕

occupational disease 職業病

employment agency 職業介紹所

22. Disasters 災難

📞 *打電話問老師問題*

1. What disasters are you familiar with?
   你知道那些災害？

2. Were you ever the victim of a disaster?
   你曾經是災害的受難者嗎？

3. Did you ever lose a loved one to a disaster?
   是否曾有你所愛的人喪生於災害中？

4. Were you ever injured in a disaster?
   你曾經在災害中受傷嗎？

5. Did you ever cause a disaster?
   你曾經引起過災難嗎？

6. How many disasters can you name?
   你能說出幾種災害來？

7. Did you ever help out in a disaster?
   你曾經在災難中幫忙嗎？

8. Can you think of any ways to avoid the occurrence of disasters?
   你能想到任何防止災難發生的方法嗎？

9. What is the difference between a natural and a man-made disaster?
   天然災害和人為災害有何不同？

📞 *打電話和老師討論問題*

Dialogue 1

老師： What disasters are you familiar with?
你知道那些災害？

學生： There are natural disasters and ***man-made disasters***. Natural disasters are phenomena such as typhoons, earthquakes and floods. Man-caused disasters are events such as fires.
有所謂的天然災害與人為災害。颱風、地震、洪水等現象是天然災害，而一些事件，如火災，屬人為災害。
➡ phenomenon (fə'namə,nan) *n*. 現象 (phenomena (fə'namənə) *pl*.)

老師： Were you ever the victim of a disaster?
你曾經是災害的受難者嗎？

學生： I was caught up in a typhoon once. I went camping with some friends, and there was a typhoon which resulted in a flood. We were stranded on a mountain for two days, but we managed to get out safely.
我曾經被颱風困住。我和一些朋友去露營，結果颱風來襲，引起洪水。我們被困在山裡兩天，不過最後平安脫困。
➡ victim ('vɪktɪm) *n*. 受害者   strand (strænd) *v*. 束手無策

老師： Did you ever lose a loved one to a disaster?
是否曾有你所愛的人喪生於災害中？

學生： No, but one of my best friends lost a cousin in a fire. She was in an illegal KTV and because the KTV was poorly designed, there was no way for her to get out. A lot of people die from fires in KTVs.
沒有，不過我有一位好友的表姊喪生於火災中。她到一家不合法的 KTV 去，由於 KTV 設計不良，她無路可逃。有許多人在 KTV 火災中罹難。

Dialogue 2

老師：Were you ever injured in a disaster?
你曾經在災害中受傷嗎？

學生：Yes. When I was trapped on the mountain in the typhoon I was talking about earlier, I sustained some light injuries. I'm glad to say that I've never been injured badly in a disaster.
是的。當我因先前提到的那次颱風而被困在山中時，我受了一點輕傷。我很慶興自己從沒在災害中受過重傷。
➔ trap〔træp〕 v. 困住　　sustain〔sə'sten〕 v. 遭受

老師：Did you ever cause a disaster? 你曾經引起過災難嗎？

學生：Of course not. I try to be careful at all times so as not to cause anything dangerous, including disasters!
當然沒有。我盡量隨時小心，不去引發危險的事情，這包括了災難。

老師：How many kinds of disasters can you name?
你能說出幾種災害來？

學生：There are earthquakes, typhoons, droughts, floods, fire, and volcanic eruptions.
地震、颱風、乾旱、洪水、火災以及火山爆發。
➔ drought〔draʊt〕 n. 旱災　　volcanic〔vɑl'kænɪk〕 adj. 火山的
eruption〔ɪ'rʌpʃən〕 n. 爆發

Dialogue 3

老師：Did you ever help out in a disaster?
你曾經在災難中幫忙嗎？

學生：I was staying overnight at my friend's house when there was a fire in an apartment nearby. Everybody, including myself, went to help.
我曾經在朋友家過夜，當時鄰近的一棟公寓發生了火災。每個人，包括我，都去幫忙。

老師： Can you think of any ways to avoid the occurrence of disasters ?

你能想到任何防止災難發生的方法嗎 ？

學生： First, we should make sure that all buildings fit safety standards and enforce them. Illegal KTVs should be closed down. There should be regular *random checks* on buildings to make sure that the rules are being obeyed.

首先，我們應該確定所有的建築物都符合、並且遵守安全標準。不合法的 KTV 應該關門、對建築物應該經常實施突擊檢查，以確保所有的規定都被遵守。

老師： What is the difference between a natural and a man-made disaster ?

天然災害和人爲災害有何不同 ？

學生： Natural disasters can be, *to some extent*, predicted. However, man-made disasters should not happen in the first place. They can be prevented if the right precautions are taken.

就某個程度來看，天然災害是可以預測的。而人爲災害最初就不該發生，如果正確的預防措施確實執行，人爲災害都可避免。

**

enforce (ɪn'fors) v. 執行　　random ('rændəm) adj. 隨意的
obey (ə'be , o'be) v. 服從　　precaution (prɪ'kɔʃən) n. 預防措施

☆ 災難相關語彙

accident (ˈæksədənt) *n.* 事故；意外

adversity (ədˈvɝsətɪ) *n.* 惡運；災難

affliction (əˈflɪkʃən) *n.* 哀傷；災難

calamity (kəˈlæmətɪ) *n.* 災難

catastrophe (kəˈtæstrəfɪ) *n.* 巨變；大災害

misadventure (ˌmɪsədˈvɛntʃɚ) *n.* 不幸事故

mischance (mɪsˈtʃæns , -ˈtʃɑns) *n.* 不幸；災難

misfortune (mɪsˈfɔrtʃən) *n.* 不幸；災難

mishap (ˈmɪsˌhæp) *n.* 不幸   blizzard (ˈblɪzɚd) *n.* 大風雪

bombing (ˈbɑmɪŋ) *n.* 轟炸   crash (kræʃ) *n.* 墜落

drought (draut) *n.* 乾旱   drowning (ˈdraunɪŋ) *n.* 溺水

hurricane (ˈhɝɪˌken) *n.* 颶風   tornado (tɔrˈnedo) *n.* 龍捲風

typhoon (taɪˈfun) *n.* 颱風

mud slide 泥流   * slide (slaɪd) *n.* 滑行

rock slide 石崩   volcano (vɑlˈkeno) *n.* 火山

lightning (ˈlaɪtnɪŋ) *n.* 閃電   hanging (ˈhæŋɪŋ) *n.* 絞死

murder (ˈmɝdɚ) *n.* 謀殺   war (wɔr) *n.* 戰爭

explosion (ɪkˈsploʒən) *n.* 爆炸

injury (ˈɪndʒərɪ) *n.* 受傷   survivor (səˈvaɪvɚ) *n.* 生還者

casualty (ˈkæʒuəltɪ) *n.* 意外事故；死傷人數 (*pl.*)

victim (ˈvɪktɪm) *n.* 犧牲者   rescue (ˈrɛskju) *n. v.* 救援

ambulance (ˈæmbjələns) *n.* 救護車

fire fighter 消防人員   red cross 紅十字

relief service 救援服務

next of kin 最近親   * kin (kɪn) *n.* 親屬

insurance (ɪnˈʃurəns) *n.* 保險

23. *Safety* 安全

📞 *打電話問老師問題*

1. How safe is the place you live?
   你住的地方安全嗎?

2. Do you know what to do in case of fire?
   萬一失火的話,你知道該怎麼辦嗎?

3. How safe is the place you work?
   你工作的地方安全嗎?

4. Do you know what to do in an emergency?
   緊急事件發生時,你知道怎麼辦嗎?

5. Have you ever left a building because you thought it was unsafe?
   你曾經因為某建築物不安全而離開嗎?

6. Would you leave a building now if you thought it was unsafe?
   現在你會因為某建築物不安全而離開嗎?

7. Do you look for exits whenever you enter a building?
   當你進入建築物時,你會尋找出口嗎?

8. Do you know what number to call in case of fire or other emergencies?
   萬一有火災或其他緊急事件發生時,你知道要打幾號嗎?

打電話和老師討論問題

Dialogue 1

老師：How safe is the place you live?
你住的地方安全嗎？

學生：I think it is one of the safest places I know. At least, the *fire escapes* are always open. But sometimes the people downstairs block it with trash. That is the most worrying thing.
我想那是我所知道最安全的地方之一，至少太平門總是敞開的。但有時候，會被樓下的人用垃圾堵住，那是最令人擔心的事。

老師：Have you ever left a building because you thought it was unsafe?
你曾經因為某建築物不安全而離開嗎？

學生：Yes. I was in a KTV a few weeks ago with a couple of friends, but we left because the fire exits were blocked.
有。前幾個禮拜我和幾個朋友在 KTV，因為火災逃生出口被堵塞而離開。

But I think that most people don't think about safety because they think accidents won't happen to them.
但是我想大多數人不會注意安全，因為他們認為意外事件不會發生在他們身上。

**　*
escape (ə'skep) *n.* 避難設施　　　　block (blɑk) *v.* 堵塞
exit ('ɛgzɪt , 'ɛksɪt) *n.* 出口

老師 : Do you know what to do in case of fire?
萬一失火的話,你知道該怎麼辦嗎?

學生 : Of course! I'd find the safest way to get out of the building and go that way. Once I am out of the building, I would *call for help*.
當然!我會找到逃出建築物最安全的一條路,然後走那條路。一旦我逃出那幢建築物,我會大呼求救。

Dialogue 2

老師 : Do you look for exits when you enter a building?
當你進入建築物時,你會去找安全門嗎?

學生 : Yes, I always do. It's a good habit and I think everyone should do it. It's the least you can do. If all the customers in an unsafe KTV left because of the blocked fire exit, then the owners would have to *do something about it*!
我一向如此。這是個好習慣,而且,我想我們都應該做,這是你僅能做的。如果所有在不安全 KTV 的顧客,能夠因為火災出口被阻塞而離開,那麼業者就非得對此採取一些措施。

老師 : Do you know the number to call in case of fire or other emergencies?
萬一有火災或其他緊急事件,你知道要打幾號嗎?

學生 : Of course. It's 119 for the fire department. Everyone should be made to learn this, even children. What about you? What do you do to ensure that you are safe?
當然知道。打一一九叫消防隊。這是每個人,甚至小孩,都得學的。你呢?你都怎麼做來確保自身的安全?

** ─────────────

call for 叫喊　　　emergency〔ɪˈmɝdʒənsɪ〕*n.* 緊急狀況

老師：I make sure that I know where all the safety exits are, and how to get to them so that when an emergency occurs, I will know exactly where the safest way out is.

我會確定自己知道所有的安全出口在那裏、怎麼走，以便在緊急事件發生時，清楚地知道那一條是最安全的逃生之路。

Dialogue 3

老師：How much do you know about safety awareness ?

關於安全意識，你的了解有多少？

學生：I always make sure if a place is safe or not whenever I enter a building. Also I try to contemplate what I will do when there is an emergency.

當我進入建築物，我一定會確認這是不是一個安全的地方，也會試想當有緊急事件時，自己該怎麼做。

老師：What do you think you will do ?

你想，你會怎麼做？

學生：The most important thing is to *remain calm*. I think this would be pretty hard if you are unprepared, but if you have already *given it some thought*, it should make things a lot easier.

最重要就是要保持鎮靜。我想如果你都沒有心理準備，這會非常困難。但如果你已經先想過，事情就會容易多了。

** ────────────

contemplate (ˈkɑntəmˌplet) v. 深思
calm (kɑm) adj. 鎮定的

老師： How safe do you think your surroundings are, in general ?

你認為你的周遭環境，一般來說安全嗎？

學生： Unfortunately, not very safe. Most of the buildings in Taiwan are fire hazards, and I think that the government should enforce the laws more strictly. Until then accidents will keep on happening.

很遺憾，不太安全。台灣大部分的建築物都有火災的危險，我認為政府應該更嚴格地執行法律，不然意外事件會一直發生。

** ————————————————

hazard (ˈhæzəd) *n.* 危險　　enforce (ɪnˈfors) *v.* 執行
strictly (ˈstrɪktlɪ) *adv.* 嚴格地

❧ 火災逃生要領 ❧

- 切莫搭乘電梯逃生，以免在密閉的空間內遭濃煙嗆傷。
- 以濕毛巾輕掩口鼻，保持呼吸順暢。
- 採低姿勢爬行逃生，呼吸地面殘留的氧氣。
- 每逃出一房間，應順手將門關上，阻絕濃煙的蔓延。
- 保持鎮定，切莫慌張。

24. *Traffic Jams* 塞車

📞 *打電話問老師問題*

1. How's the traffic in the city you live?
   你居住的城市交通如何？

2. How do you go to school / work?
   你如何上學/上班？

3. How long does it take you to go to school / work?
   你上學/上班要花多久時間？

4. What brings about serious traffic jams?
   為什麼會造成嚴重的交通阻塞？

5. What's the cost of traffic jams?
   交通阻塞會讓我們付出何種代價？

6. What do you do when you are caught in traffic jams?
   當你困在車陣中時，你會怎麼辦？

7. Do you have a Mass Rapid Transit System?
   你們有大眾捷運系統嗎？

8. Is there any solution to the traffic problems?
   交通問題有什麼解決之道嗎？

9. Have you ever suffered a loss of any kind as a result of getting caught in a traffic jam?
   你曾經因為塞車而蒙受損失嗎？

📞 *打電話和老師討論問題*

Dialogue 1

老師 : How's the traffic in the city you live?
你居住的城市交通如何?

學生 : It's very bad. I think the traffic in Taipei is some of the worst in Asia. During *rush hour*, it is sometimes quicker to walk! The thing which really annoys me is watching pedestrians overtaking me while I am *stuck in a traffic jam*.
很差。我想一定是全亞洲最糟之一。在尖峰時間,有時候用走的反而來得快!每當陷在車陣當中,卻看見行人一個個追過我,真是令人生氣。

→ *rush hour* (交通)尖峰時間　　pedestrian (pəˈdɛstrɪən) *n.* 行人
overtake (ˌovəˈtek) *v.* 追過

老師 : How do you go to school / work?
你如何上學/上班?

學生 : I use public transportation. The buses come frequently but can get very crowded. I think it is a fair service, and the fare is certainly cheap.
我搭乘大眾運輸工具。公車的班次很頻繁,但是有時候很擁擠。我認為這是個很好的服務,公車票價十分便宜。

→ transportation (ˌtrænspəˈteʃən) *n.* 運輸工具　　fare (fɛr) *n.* 車資

老師 : How long does it take you to go to school / work?
你上學/上班要花多久的時間?

學生 : It usually takes between half an hour and forty-five minutes, depending on *traffic flow*. If there is no traffic, it only takes 20 minutes.
通常是半小時到四十五分鐘,要視交通流量而定。如果沒什麼車,只需要二十分鐘。

Dialogue 2

老師：What brings about serious traffic jams?
為什麼會造成嚴重的交通阻塞？

學生：Various factors *contribute to* this problem. There are too many vehicles for the roads to accommodate, the construction of the MRT worsens this, and also illegal parking restricts traffic flow.
造成這個問題的原因有好幾個。車輛太多了，道路根本就容納不下，捷運的工程使得問題更加惡化，而違規停車更限制了車流量。

老師：What's the cost of traffic jams?
交通阻塞會讓我們付出何種代價？

學生：The financial costs are perhaps more than one would think. People will be late for appointments, for work and for school.
財務上的損失可能遠超過我們所能想像的。大家約會、上班、上學都會遲到。

Being stuck in a traffic jam increases stress, and the longer your car is turned on, the more toxic emissions it will produce.
塞在車陣中會增加人們的壓力，而車子開愈久，車子排放的有毒物質就愈多。

**
contribute (kən'trɪbjut) *v.* 助成；促成
vehicle ('viɪkḷ) *n.* 車輛
accommodate (ə'kɑmə,det) *v.* 容納
restrict (rɪ'strɪkt) *v.* 限制
toxic ('tɑksɪk) *adj.* 有毒的   emission (ɪ'mɪʃən) *n.* 排放

老師：What do you do when you are caught in a traffic jam?
當你困在車陣中時，你會怎麼辦？

學生：If I am on a bus and the situation is really bad, I will
get off the bus and walk; if I am in a car, I will try to
find an alternative route.
如果我在公車上，而情況眞的很糟的話，我會下車用走的；如果我自
己開車，我會改道行駛。

Dialogue 3

老師：Do you have a Mass Rapid Transit System?
你們有捷運嗎？

學生：No, but one is being built. It is designed to *relieve
congestion*, but right now it's making it worse!
沒有，但正在建造中。這項捷運工程當初設計的目的，是要紓解
交通阻塞，但是現在情況卻更惡化了。

老師：Is there any solution to the traffic problems?
交通問題有什麼解決之道嗎？

學生：Wider roads would definitely be of use. More money
should be spent on transport police, who should take
a tougher stance on illegal parking. This is hard because space is restricted in big cities.
道路加寬一定會有用的。應該增加更多經費補助交通警察，更嚴格
取締違規停車。這十分困難，因爲大城市裡的空間十分有限。

** ──────────

alternative (ɔl'tɝnətɪv) *adj.* 另一個可選的
transit ('trænsɪt, -zɪt) *n.* 運送   relieve (rɪ'liv) *v.* 緩和
congestion (kən'dʒɛstʃən) *n.* 交通阻塞
take a ~ stance 採取~立場

老師：Have you ever suffered a loss of any kind as a result of getting caught in a traffic jam?

你曾經因為塞車而蒙受損失嗎？

學生：There was once when I was supposed to meet my date at 6 p.m. But because there was a traffic jam I was half an hour late, and my date never forgave me for that!

有一次我要赴晚上六點鐘的約。但是因為交通阻塞，遲到了半小時，而和我約會的人，一直都不肯原諒我。

**

date〔det〕*n.* 相與約會之人

☆ 塞車相關語彙

traffic ticket 交通罰單

commuter〔kə'mjutə〕*n.* 通勤者

carpool 共乘　　　　　　scooter〔'skutə〕*n.* 摩托車

give *sb.* a lift 搭載某人　hitchhike〔'hɪtʃ,haɪk〕*v.* 搭便車

run through the red light 闖紅燈

parking lot 停車位

honk〔haŋk〕*v.* 按喇叭　　honk the horn 按喇叭

The traffic is bumper to bumper. 車子大排長龍

　* bumper〔'bʌmpə〕*n.* 保險桿

25. *Smoking* 吸 煙

📞 *打電話問老師問題*

1. Do you have any experiences with smoking?
   你有抽煙的經驗嗎？

2. Would you ever smoke? 你以後會抽煙嗎？

3. Are you aware of the consequences that smoking can bring about?
   你知道抽煙所造成的後果嗎？

4. Do you know of a good way to quit smoking?
   你知道戒煙的好方法嗎？

5. Have you ever known anyone who has successfully quit smoking?
   你認識的人當中，有誰戒煙成功？

6. Do you have anyone in your family who smokes?
   你們家有人抽煙嗎？

7. What would you say is a good way of countering the the public from smoking too much?
   你認為要防止大家抽煙過度最好的方法是什麼？

8. How many people in your school smoke?
   你們學校有多少人會抽煙？

9. What is the cost to the average smoker annually?
   一般的抽煙者每年要花多少錢？

📞 *打電話和老師討論問題*

Dialogue 1

老師： Do you have any experiences with smoking?
你有抽煙的經驗嗎?

學生： Cigarettes have been offered to me, but luckily I declined. I don't know what the consequences would have been had I accepted.
曾有人遞煙給我,但幸運的是,我拒絕了。當初我要是接受的話,不知道會有什麼後果。

老師： Do you have any other experiences with smoking?
你有任何其他抽煙的經驗嗎?

學生： I was at a disco party, and some friends who were smoking offered me some cigarettes.
我曾參加一個迪斯可舞會,有些抽煙的朋友遞給我一些香煙。

老師： They can't be your good friends if they offer you cigarettes!
如果他們給你煙的話,那就不算是什麼好朋友了。

學生： Actually I am not really very well *acquainted with* them. I have only known them for less than a month.
事實上我和他們並不熟,我們認識才不到一個月。

** ───────────

decline〔dɪ'klaɪn〕*v.* 拒絕
consequence〔'kɑnsə,kwɛns〕*n.* 後果
acquainted〔ə'kwentɪd〕*adj.* 認識的

Dialogue 2

老師 : Are you aware of the consequences that smoking can bring about ?

你知道抽煙會造成什麼後果嗎？

學生 : Of course. The nicotine found in cigarettes induces a relaxing sensation and puts the smoker in a "happier" mood. Smokers develop a craving for nicotine, and that's when they're addicted.

當然知道。香煙裡的尼古丁會產生一種令人放鬆的感覺，而且會使吸煙者心情變得更愉快。吸煙者會產生對尼古丁的一種渴望，這時候他們就上癮了。

老師 : Have you ever known anyone who has successfully quit smoking ?

你認識戒煙成功的人嗎？

學生 : Actually most of the people I know who tried to quit never succeeded. However, my uncle did successfully quit.

事實上，我認識的人當中，想戒煙的大多失敗了。然而，我的叔叔戒煙卻很成功。

He went to see the doctor after he had a stroke, and the doctor said that it would be best if he quit. And he did !

他中風之後去看醫生，醫生建議他最好要戒煙，而他真的做到了！

**

nicotine (ˈnɪkəˌtin) *n.* 尼古丁   induce (ɪnˈdjus) *v.* 引起
sensation (sɛnˈseʃən) *n.* 感覺   craving (ˈkrevɪŋ) *n.* 渴望
stroke (strok) *n.* 中風

老師：Do you know of a good way to quit smoking？
你知道戒煙的好方法嗎？

學生：The best way to stop is to never start. If you have already started, I think the best way to quit is to have the determination to quit and also to seek proper counseling.
最好是一開始就不要抽煙。如果已經開始抽煙的話，那麼戒煙最好的方法是要有決心，而且要尋求一些適當的輔導。

Dialogue 3

老師：Do you have anyone in your family who smokes？
你們家有人抽煙嗎？

學生：The only one in my family who smokes is my father. But I think that is *due to* the stress he gets from working. Chinese people are always having official dinners when you have to drink and smoke excessively！
我們家只有我父親會抽煙。但我認為那是因為他工作時的壓力所造成的。中國人常有一些應酬，在這些場合中都會過度飲酒與抽煙。

老師：What would you say is a good way of countering the public from smoking too much？
你認為要防止大家抽煙過度最好的方法是什麼？

學生：The public should be made more aware of the dreadful consequences of smoking, such as lung cancer or heart failure.
應該使大眾了解抽煙的可怕後果，像是肺癌與心臟病。

＊＊ ──────────────

counseling (ˈkaʊnslɪŋ) *n.* 輔導　　stress (strɛs) *n.* 壓力
excessively (ɪkˈsɛsɪvlɪ) *adv.* 過度地　　counter (ˈkaʊntɚ) *v.* 對抗
dreadful (ˈdrɛdfəl) *adj.* 可怕的　　*heart failure* 心臟病

老師： How many people in your school smoke？
你們學校裡有多少人抽煙？

學生： Many do. I think students smoke because they want
to be adults, and they like the "cool" image *associated with* smoking. Students don't really think too
much about their long-term health because they are
too young.

很多。我認爲學生抽煙是因爲他們想成爲大人，喜歡與香煙有關的
「很酷的」形象。學生不太會考慮自己身體長期的健康，因爲他們
太年輕了。

** ─────────────────────
image（'ɪmɪdʒ）*n.* 形象

☆ 吸煙相關語彙

---

chainsmoker（'tʃɛn'smokɚ）*n.* 老煙槍

cigar（sɪ'gɑr）*n.* 雪茄   nonsmoker 不抽煙者

secondhand smoke 二手煙   sidestream smoke 二手煙

butt（bʌt）*n.* 煙蒂

puff（pʌf）*v.* 一口接一口地吸煙；吹出煙

inhale（ɪn'hel）*v.* 吸入   snuff（snʌf）*v.* 以鼻子吸；熄掉

emphysema（,ɛmfə'simə）*n.* 肺氣腫

pulmonary（'pʌlmə,nɛrɪ）*adj.* 肺的

ban（bæn）*n.* 禁止   prohibit（pro'hɪbɪt）*v.* 禁止

outlaw（'aut,lɔ）*v.* 宣告非法；禁止

penalize（'pɛnḷ,aɪz）*v.* 處罰

tobacco（tə'bæko）*n.* 菸草   alcohol（'ælkə,hɔl）*n.* 酒精飲料

26. Drug Abuse 吸 毒

📞 打電話問老師問題

1. What do you know about drug abuse?
   你對毒品泛濫的情況了解多少?

2. Do you know what types of drugs there are?
   你知道毒品有那幾種嗎?

3. Can you give me an example of a soft drug?
   你能舉個溫和毒品的例子嗎?

4. What about hard drugs?　那強烈的毒品又如何呢?

5. Do you know the seriousness of these hard drugs?
   你知道這些強烈毒品的嚴重性嗎?

6. Where do you think the kids are getting these drugs
   from?　你認為孩子的毒品是那兒來的?

7. How widespread is the problem of drugs for young
   people today?
   現在青少年的毒品問題已擴大到何種程度?

8. What do you think can be done about drug abuse?
   你認為該如何處理毒品氾濫?

9. Does anyone you know use drugs?
   你認識的人中,有人吸毒嗎?

📞 *打電話和老師討論問題*

Dialogue 1

老師：What do you know about drug abuse?
你對毒品泛濫的情況了解多少？

學生：I know enough about drug abuse not to touch them!
Most drugs are harmful and that includes the nicotine
in cigarettes!
我很了解，知道不可去接觸它們。大部分的毒品都是有害的，甚至
連香煙裡的尼古丁也不例外。

老師：Do you know what types of drugs there are?
你知道毒品有那幾種嗎？

學生：There are generally two types of drugs, that people
term as soft and hard drugs.
通常毒品可分爲兩種，一般人將其歸類爲溫和與強烈的毒品。

Soft drugs are recreational drugs which give you a
light-headed feeling and a general feeling of well-
being. They are considered as non-addictive.
溫和的毒品是供娛樂用的，會令人覺得頭昏昏的，通常會有種幸福
的感覺，一般認爲這種毒品是不會上癮的。

**

abuse (ə'bjus) *n.* 濫用
nicotine ('nɪkə,tin) *n.* 尼古丁
recreational (,rɛkrɪ'eʃənḷ) *adj.* 休閒的；娛樂的
light-headed ('laɪt'hɛdɪd) *adj.* 頭昏眼花的
well-being ('wɛl'biɪŋ) *n.* 幸福
non-addictive (,nɑn ə'dɪktɪv) *adj.* 不會使人上癮的

老師： Give me an example of a soft drug.
請舉個例子說明溫和的毒品。

學生： Most of the soft drugs found today are derivatives of the hemp plant, known as cannabis. It's generally known as marijuana which is the Mexican word for cannabis. It can be refined into a form known as hashish.

現在溫和的毒品，大部分都是大麻植物，也就是印度大麻的衍生物。墨西哥人稱印度大麻爲大麻煙，這是一般人所知道的稱呼。它可以提煉成一種麻醉藥。

Dialogue 2

老師： What about hard drugs？
那強烈的毒品又如何呢？

學生： You have ecstasy tablets, LSD, cocaine and heroin. They are all very dangerous and potentially lethal. The two most dangerous are cocaine, also known as Coke, and heroin. They are very addictive and *once you start, you can't stop*.

強烈的毒品有興奮劑、迷幻藥、古柯鹼和海洛因，這些都具有危險性，而且可能會致命。最危險的兩種是古柯鹼，又名 Coke，以及海洛因。這兩種會使人上癮，而且一旦開始服用，就很難停止。

**

derivative〔dəˈrɪvətɪv〕*n.* 衍生物　　hemp〔hɛmp〕*n.* 大麻
cannabis〔ˈkænəbɪs〕*n.* 印度大麻　　marijuana〔͵mærəˈwɑnə〕*n.* 大麻煙
refine〔rɪˈfaɪn〕*v.* 提煉　　hashish〔ˈhæʃiʃ〕*n.* 印度大麻葉製造的一種麻醉藥
ecstasy〔ˈɛkstəsɪ〕*n.* 欣喜若狂　　tablet〔ˈtæblɪt〕*n.* 藥片
LSD〔ˈɛl͵ɛsˈdi〕*n.* 一種迷幻藥　（ *lysergic acid dielhylamide* ）
cocaine〔koˈken〕*n.* 古柯鹼　　heroin〔ˈhɛroɪn〕*n.* 海洛因
lethal〔ˈliθəl〕*adj.* 致命的

老師 : Do you know the seriousness of these hard drugs ?
你知道這些強烈毒品的嚴重性嗎？

學生 : When the users are addicted and crave for more, they will do anything to *get hold of* more drugs. This would include robbing people for money and doing anything the dealers tell them to do.
當服用毒品的人上癮了，並且想要更多的毒品時，他們會不顧一切去做任何事。他們可能會去搶別人的錢，做一些毒品販子要他們做的事。
➡ crave〔krev〕*v.* 渴望　　*get hold of* 獲得
　dealer〔'dilɚ〕*n.* 銷售者

老師 : You're right. This is a very serious problem, and the problem doesn't even stop there.
你說的沒錯，這是個非常嚴重的問題，而且問題還不只如此。

學生 : No, the addicts effectively become the slaves of the dealers and do whatever they are told, including murder. The pitiful thing is that society seems to punish the addicts more than the dealers, where the real root of evil is.
沒錯，有毒癮的人的確會成為毒販的奴隸，並且會對他們言聽計從，包括去殺人。令人遺憾的是，社會對吸毒者的處罰，似乎比販賣毒品的這些罪魁禍首，還要嚴厲。

Dialogue 3

老師 : How widespread do you think the problem of drugs is for young people today ?
你認為現在年輕人的毒品問題有多嚴重？

學生 : I think it is a problem which is on the increase, even as we speak ! This is something which definitely needs to be addressed.
我認為這個問題已日益嚴重，即使我們在談話時也不例外！這的確是個值得提出來的問題。

老師： Where do you think the kids are getting these drugs from?

你認為孩子們的毒品是從那裡來的？

學生： *As far as I know*, the kids are getting introduced to these things at parties where they are approached by dealers and given free drugs. Then once these kids become dependent, they pay whatever price the dealers ask for.

據我所知，毒販會利用舞會接近並認識這些孩子，然後再給他們免費的毒品。一旦孩子們對這些毒品產生依賴時，不管毒販要求什麼價錢，他們都會照付。

老師： What do you think can be done about it?

你認為該如何處理這件事？

學生： I think the relevant authorities and the government should send qualified personnel to all schools and colleges, and *give talks on* the truth about drug addiction. Then there should be help-lines giving guidance to those who most need it.

我認為有關當局與政府應該派遣合格的人員，到所有的學校與大專院校，告訴大家染上毒癮的真實後果。而且也該設立協助專線，提供指導給那些迫切需要幫助的人。

** ─────────────────────────

relevant (ˈrɛləvənt) *adj.* 有關聯的　　authorities (əˈθɔrətɪz) *n. pl.* 當局
personnel (ˌpɜsn̩ˈɛl) *n.* 人員　　guidance (ˈgaɪdəns) *n.* 輔導

27. *Young People* 新人類

📞 *打電話問老師問題*

1. What opinions do you have about the state of the youth in your country today?
   對於你們國內現在年輕人的情況，你有什麼看法？

2. How well do you think the youth are coping with the problem you just mentioned?
   對於你剛提到的問題，你覺得年輕人處理得怎樣？

3. What do you think should be done about the education system in Taiwan? 你認為台灣的教育體制應該要做何改善？

4. What kinds of things do young people do in their free time? 年輕人空閒時都做那些事？

5. Do you have free time during your holidays to do things that you like? 放假時，你有空做你喜歡的事嗎？

6. Do you think more leisure time should be made for teen-agers so that they have more time to follow their interests?
   你認為該給青少年更多的閒暇時間，讓他們有空可以從事自己感興趣的事嗎？

7. Do you think that today's youth are being treated fairly?
   你認為現今的年輕人受到公平的待遇嗎？

8. Are you happy being a young person?
   身為年輕人你覺得快樂嗎？

9. What do you expect the youth will be like in tomorrow's society? 你對將來社會上的年輕人有何期許？

📞 打電話和老師討論問題

Dialogue 1

老師：What opinions do you have about the state of the youth in Taiwan today?
對於台灣現在年輕人的情況，你有什麼看法？

學生：I think there is a lot of pressure on kids in Taiwan today. They are under pressure from the schools, parents, and even themselves.
我認為今天在台灣的小孩受到很多壓力。他們要承受來自學校、家長甚至他們自身所給予的壓力。

老師：How well do you think the youth are coping with the pressure? 你認為年輕人面對壓力應付得好不好？

學生：Most people simply live with it and try to make the best of the situation. They **hold out** and wait until they hit college! Others can't and become resigned. This is a serious problem.
大多數人就是面對問題，並且盡力而為；他們會忍耐等待，直到進入大學。有些人辦不到，於是就聽天由命了，這是個嚴重的問題。
→ **hold out** 堅持　　resign〔rɪˋzaɪn〕v. 聽任

老師：What do you think should be done about the education system in Taiwan?
你認為台灣的教育體制應該要做何改善？

學生：I think the authorities should stop talking and assess the situation carefully, and then, after coming up with a feasible plan, **put it into practice**. Phase out the existing exam system gradually and introduce a new one.
我認為當局應該停止大放厥辭，仔細評估情況，然後提出可行的計畫付諸實行。逐漸廢止現行考試制度，引用新的制度。
→ assess〔əˋsɛs〕v. 評估　　feasible〔ˋfizəbḷ〕adj. 可實行的

Dialogue 2

老師 : What kinds of things do young people do in their free time ?

年輕人空閒時都做些什麼？

學生 : They don't really have much free time. They have to go to school six days a week, and most people go to cram schools in the evening and weekends. *As a result*, a lot of people sleep in their free time!

事實上，他們的空閒時間不多。一個星期有六天要上學，而且大多數學生晚上和週末都要補習。所以，很多人有空時都在睡覺。

老師 : Do you think that more time should be made for teenagers so that they have more time to follow their interests ?

你認爲該給青少年更多的閒暇時間，讓他們有空可以從事自己感興趣的事嗎？

學生 : Of course I do! Every young person today would. I think we should follow the West and have Saturdays school-free. That way they will have more time to do what they want. But this is something which is very difficult to implement.

當然啦！現在每個年輕人都這麼認爲。我認爲我們應該向西方國家學習星期六不上課，那樣他們就會有更多時間做想做的事，不過這是很難實現的。

**
cram school 補習班   *as a result* 因此
implement ('ɪmplə,mɛnt) *v.* 實行

老師： Do you have free time during your holidays to do things that you like ? 放假時，你有空做自己喜歡的事嗎？

學生： I normally go mountain climbing with my friends if I have a Sunday off. Otherwise I may go and see a movie. I rarely go to KTVs because I have a Laser-disc machine in my house, and a lot of KTVs are fire hazards.

星期天放假時，我通常和朋友一起去爬山，要不然就去看電影。我很少去 KTV，因爲我家就有影碟機，而且很多 KTV 都有火災的危險。

→ hazard (ˊhæzə-d) *n.* 危險

Dialogue 3

老師： Do you think that today's youth are being treated fairly ? 你認爲現今的年輕人受到公平的待遇嗎？

學生： Not really. The young people today are all students and are expected to do nothing but study. This is the role that society has put upon them, and there is little concern for their other interests!

實際上沒有，現在的年輕人都是學生，被要求除了讀書外，什麼事都不用做。這就是社會加諸他們的角色，一點都不關心他們其他的興趣。

老師： So in general are you happy being a young person ? 那麼平心而論，身爲年輕人你覺得快樂嗎？

學生： I am. The adults are always saying how much they admire us because we are young , but conversely most of the young people can't wait to become adults. Part of this is a craving for freedom. Personally, I'm pretty happy with being young.

是的。大人總是說有多羨慕我們，因爲我們年輕；可是大部分年輕人反而等不及想變成大人，這多半是出自對自由的渴望。我個人是非常高興身爲一個年輕人。

→ conversely (kənˊvɜslɪ) *adv.* 相反地

老師： What do you expect the youth will be like in tomorrow's society ?

你對將來社會上的年輕人有何期許？

學生： I'd hope that there would be less pressure from all sides to study, and that there would be more space for us to do what we want, be it sports or whatever. I'd like to see more youngsters taking part in *volunteer work*, too.

我希望各方面課業的壓力能減少，讓我們有更多的空間，做我們想做的事，像是運動或諸如此類。我也樂見更多年輕人加入義工行列。

**
youngster (ˈjʌŋstɚ) *n.* 青少年
volunteer (ˌvɑlənˈtɪr) *adj.* 志願的

28. *Election* 選 舉

📞 *打電話問老師問題*

1. What elections do you have in your country?
   你們國家有那些選舉?

2. When are the elections held? 選舉什麼時候舉行?

3. What are your elections like?
   你們的選舉情形如何?

4. What main political parties are there running in your country? 你們國內有那些主要政黨?

5. What are the strategies of each main party?
   每個主要政黨的政見是什麼?

6. During elections is there a lot of advertising in the streets? 選舉時有很多的街頭宣傳活動嗎?

7. Has there been any changes in the ways in which people vote? 人們選舉的方式是否有所改變?

8. Is vote-buying widespread in your country?
   買票在你們國家很普遍嗎?

9. How bad is the situation with vote-buying in your country?
   你們國內買票的情況有多糟糕?

10. Do you think the election system is good enough in your country? 你覺得你們國家的選舉制度夠完善嗎?

📞 打電話和老師討論問題

Dialogue 1

老師： When were the legislative elections held？
立法委員選舉何時舉行？

學生： The latest legislative elections were held on December 2nd, 1995, and the presidential elections were held on March 23th, 1996.
最近一次的立委選舉是在一九九五年十二月二日舉辦，總統選舉則在一九九六年三月二十三日舉行。

➡ legislative (ˈlɛdʒɪsˌletɪv) *adj.* 立法的
presidential (ˌprɛzəˈdɛnʃəl) *adj.* 總統的

老師： What were the legislative elections like？
立委選舉情形如何？

學生： The latest ones were a bit of a surprise because the streets were less busy. In past years, you could see *a sea of people* with banners, but this time it wasn't so apparent. There was also less corporate backing.
最近這一次有點出人意料，因為街上沒有以前熱鬧。往年的話，你可以看到群眾揮舞著旗幟，但是這一次較不明顯，而且也很少有團體在聲援。

➡ banner (ˈbænə) *n.* 旗幟　　corporate (ˈkɔrp(ə)rɪt) *n.* 團體的

老師： Why was there less advertising in the streets in the legislative elections of 1995？
為什麼一九九五年的立委選舉，街頭上的宣傳活動比較少呢？

學生： The growing number of cable channels has meant that candidates are now advertising on cable. Also, there are not as many "star candidates" this time.
有線電視頻道的蓬勃發展，意味著候選人可以在電視上宣傳。此外，這次也沒有太多的「明星候選人」出馬競選。

➡ advertising (ˈædvəˌtaɪzɪŋ) *n.* 宣傳　　candidate (ˈkændəˌdet) *n.* 候選人

老師： What's the significance of the presidential elections ?
這次的總統選舉有何意義？

學生： This is the first time in the history of the Republic of China, in which the people of Taiwan could choose their own president.
這是中華民國史上，台灣人民第一次可以自己選總統。

老師： Why did Lee win the elections ?
爲什麼李登輝能贏得這次選舉？

學生： He won because of a number of reasons. He had been *in office* for eight years and was the most qualified for the job. The Mainland government didn't want Lee to be elected and used missiles to scare the Taiwanese, but this had a reverse effect; the residents of Taiwan became more united and Lee won with a larger margin than expected.
他能獲勝有一些原因。他在位已經八年，所以是最適任這個職位的人。大陸政府不希望李登輝當選，使用飛彈恫嚇台灣人，但是卻收到反效果。台灣的人民變得更團結，使得李登輝高票當選，超出原先所預期。
→ missile（ˈmɪsl̩）*n.* 飛彈　　reverse（rɪˈvɝs）*adj.* 相反的

Dialogue 2

老師： What are the main political parties in Taiwan ?
台灣有那些大的政黨？

學生： The *ruling party* is the Kuomintang（KMT）, and the main opposition is the Democratic Progressive Party （DPP）, formed 9 years ago. The third largest party is the New Party. It was formed just 2 years ago by some stray KMT members.
執政黨是國民黨，而主要的在野黨爲民主進步黨，它於九年前成立。第三大黨是新黨，是由二年前出走的國民黨員所組成。
→ opposition（ˌɑpəˈzɪʃən）*n.* 反對　　democratic（ˌdɛməˈkrætɪk）*adj.* 民主的
progressive（prəˈgrɛsɪv）*adj.* 進步的　　stray（stre）*adj.* 分散的

老師：What are the strategies of each party?
每個政黨的主要政見是什麼？

學生：The KMT is playing the "stability and welfare" card, which in the past has been pretty effective. The DPP is taking a reform and pro-independence stance. The New Party is taking an anti-corruption stance and making a claim for the defence of the R.O.C. government.
國民黨打的是「安定和富裕」牌，這在以往都相當有效。民進黨採取的是改革和台獨姿態；新黨主張的是反貪污、捍衛中華民國。

→ strategy ('strætədʒɪ) *n.* 策略　　stability (stə'bɪlətɪ) *n.* 安定
welfare ('wɛl,fɛr , -fær) *n.* 福利　　reform (rɪ'form) *n.* 改革
independence (,ɪndɪ'pɛndəns) *n.* 獨立　　stance (stæns) *n.* 姿態；態度
corruption (kə'rʌpʃən) *n.* 貪污　　claim (klem) *n.* 主張

老師：Has there been any changes in the ways people vote?
人們選舉的方式是否有所改變？

學生：In the past, the people used to just vote for the candidate that they liked, but nowadays people *take into consideration* the party which the candidate belongs to.
在以往，人們通常只選他們所喜歡的候選人，可是現在也會考慮候選人所屬的政黨。

→ vote (vot) *v. n.* 投票　　consideration (kən,sɪdə'reʃən) *n.* 考慮

Dialogue 3

老師：Just how bad is the situation with vote-buying in Taiwan? 在台灣，買票的情況有多糟呢？

學生：In the past, a lot of candidates who had money would bribe voters with red envelopes, to ensure victory. Now bribing voters is no longer a way to ensure votes because more people have their own political beliefs.
以前，很多有錢的候選人為了當選，都會送紅包，賄賂選民。現在，賄賂選民已不能確保選票，因為愈來愈多人有自己的政治理念。

→ bribe (braɪb) *v.* 賄賂　　ensure (ɪn'ʃur) *v.* 確定；保證

老師： Is vote-buying still widespread？
買票仍然很普遍嗎？

學生： It's still there, even though it's not as bad as what it used to be. A lot of candidates were accused of vote-buying in the 1995 legislative elections.
雖然沒有像以前那麼嚴重，但仍然存在。一九九五年立委選舉期間，很多候選人也因買票而被告發。
→ accuse〔ə'kjuz〕v. 控訴；告發

老師： Do you think the election system is good enough in Taiwan？
你認爲台灣的選舉制度夠完善嗎？

學生： It certainly is improving, but there are still more things to be done. But it is good to see that at least we're improving. We still have ways to go, and a lot more work to do.
確實有在改善，但仍有許多事情待做。不過，很高興看到我們至少有在改進。我們還有路要走，還有工作要做。

☆ **選舉相關語彙**

Legislative Yuan 立法院
legislature〔'lɛdʒɪs,letʃɚ〕n. 立法機關
legislator〔'lɛdʒɪs,letɚ〕n. 立法委員　　　　lawmaker 立法人員
parliament〔'parləmənt〕n. 國會
candidate〔'kændə,det,'kændədɪt〕n. 候選人
nominee〔,namə'ni〕n. 被提名人
nomination〔,namə'neʃən〕n. 提名

representative (ˌrɛprɪˈzɛntətɪv) *n.* 代表

councilor (ˈkaʊnslʒ) *n.* 議員　　mayor (ˈmeə , mɛr) *n.* 市長

premier (ˈprimɪə) *n.* 行政院長　　Cabinet (ˈkæbənɪt) *n.* 內閣

vote (vot) *v. n.* 投票；選票　　voter (ˈvotə) *n.* 選舉人

poll (pol) *n.* 投票；投票結果；民意調查

polls (*pl.*) 投票所　　polling station 投票所

ballot (ˈbælət) *n.* 選票　*v.* 投票

electorate (ɪˈlɛktərɪt) *n.* 選民；選舉區

constituency (kənˈstɪtʃʊənsɪ) *n.* 選舉區

incumbent (ɪnˈkʌmbənt) *adj.* 現任的

contender (kənˈtɛndə) *n.* 競爭對手

campaign (kæmˈpen) *n.* 活動

seat (sit) *n.* 席次　　vote-share 得票率

bribe (braɪb) *v.* 賄賂　　bribery (ˈbraɪbərɪ) *n.* 賄賂

golden oxen 金牛　　vote-rationing 配票

crack down 取締　　veteran (ˈvɛtərən) *n.* 老兵；榮民

veteran home 榮民之家　　observer (əbˈzɜvə) *n.* 觀察家

analyst (ˈænḷɪst) *n.* 分析家　　coalition (ˌkoəˈlɪʃən) *n.* 聯合政治

victory (ˈvɪkt(ə)rɪ) *n.* 勝利　　setback (ˈsɛtˌbæk) *n.* 挫敗

veto (ˈvito) *n. v.* 否決　　opposition party 在野黨

ruling party 執政黨　　press conference 記者會

the Ministry of Justice 法務部

identity card 身分證　　chop (tʃap) *n.* 印章

seal (sil) *n.* 印章

29. *Beauty Contest* 選 美

📞 *打電話問老師問題*

1. Do you like to watch beauty contests ?
   你喜歡看選美比賽嗎？

2. Do you think that most beauty contestants are really beautiful ? 你認為選美的大部分參賽者真的漂亮嗎？

3. Do you think beauty contestants are smart ?
   你認為選美的參賽者聰明嗎？

4. Do you think it is important for beauty contests to have a talent section ?
   你認為選美比賽中，才藝表演這個項目很重要嗎？

5. Do you think beauty contestants should wear swim suits during part of the contest ?
   你認為選美比賽中，參賽者應該穿泳裝嗎？

6. Do you usually agree with the judges' choice of the winner for a beauty contest ?
   選美比賽中，評審所選出的優勝者，你同意嗎？

7. Do you know anyone who has entered a beauty contest ?
   你認識什麼人參加過選美比賽嗎？

8. Would you ever enter a beauty contest ? 你會參加選美比賽嗎？

9 Would you let your daughter enter a beauty contest ?
   你會讓你的女兒參加選美比賽嗎？

📞 *打電話和老師討論問題*

Dialogue 1

老師：Do you like to watch beauty contests？
你喜歡看選美比賽嗎？

學生：Sometimes. I like to watch beauty contests with friends. Then we can *comment on* the contestants.
有時候會。我喜歡和朋友一起看選美比賽，然後我們會對那些參賽者品頭論足。

老師：Do you think beauty contestants are really beautiful？
你認為選美比賽的參賽者真的漂亮嗎？

學生：It depends on how big the contest is. The girls in the large beauty contest are mostly beautiful, while some of the girls in the smaller ones are not very pretty.
那要看比賽的規模有多大。大型比賽中的參賽小姐，大部分都很漂亮，而小一點的比賽中，有些就不是很漂亮了。

老師：Do you think beauty contestants are smart？
你認為選美的參賽者聰明嗎？

學生：I suppose some of them are. You can tell how smart they are during the question answering part of the contest.
我想有些是很聰明，你可以從她們在比賽中，回答問題時看出來。

**
comment ('kɑmɛnt) *v.* 評論
contestant (kən'tɛstənt) *n.* 參賽者

Dialogue 2

老師：Do you think it is important for beauty contests to have a talent section ?

你認為選美比賽中，才藝表演這個項目很重要嗎？

學生：Of course. Beauty without talent is useless. You can be born with a pretty face, but talent is acquired through work.

當然。空有美貌但沒有智慧是沒用的。你可能與生俱來一張漂亮的臉蛋，但智慧是從工作中學習獲得。

老師：Do you think beauty contestants should wear swim suits during part of the contest ?

你認為選美比賽中，參賽者應該穿泳裝嗎？

學生：I think so. In order to be a truly beautiful person you must be beautiful both outside and inside. And beauty on the outside is best judged when the contestants wear swim suits.

我是這麼認為。想成為一個真正的美人，你必須內外皆美。當參賽者穿上泳裝時，是評審外在美最好的辦法。

老師：Do you usually agree with the judges' choice of the winner for a beauty contest ?

選美比賽中，評審所選出的優勝者，你同意嗎？

學生：Actually I rarely do. Most of the time when I see a contest on TV, the ones I think should win never do. I think everyone has different tastes, so you can't expect the judges to agree with you all the time.

事實上我很少贊同。大部分我在電視上所看到的比賽，我認為應該獲勝的從來就沒贏過。我覺得每個人的品味不同，你不可能期望評審每一次的看法都和你相同。

Dialogue 3

老師： Do you know anyone who's entered a beauty contest?
你認識什麼人參加過選美比賽嗎？

學生： Yes. Some of my friends enter beauty contests all the time. They get on television quite often.
有，我的一些朋友老是去參加選美比賽，她們常常上電視。

老師： Would you ever enter a beauty contest?
你會參加選美比賽嗎？

學生： I wouldn't, even if I had the looks. The chance of winning is slim, and the winners usually enter the *entertainment industry* such as acting. I don't think I can cope with facing *the press* and all the publicity. I'd have no private life at all!
才不會，即使我的長相不錯。獲勝的機會很渺茫，而且優勝者常會進入娛樂圈，像是演藝界。我不認為我可以應付媒體和大眾，我會完全喪失隱私權。

老師： Would you let your daughter enter a beauty contest?
你會讓你的女兒參加選美比賽嗎？

學生： If she wanted to, I'd let her. I don't think there's any harm in beauty contests.
如果她要去的話，我會讓她去。我不認為選美比賽有什麼害處。

**
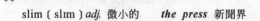

slim〔slɪm〕*adj.* 微小的　　*the press* 新聞界

30. Religion 宗教

📞 *打電話問老師問題*

1. Are you a religious person？你信仰宗教虔誠嗎？

2. What is your religion？你信仰什麼宗教？

3. Why do you follow your religion？
   你為何信仰這個宗教？

4. Do you attend religious services often？
   你常參加宗教儀式嗎？

5. Do you pray often？你常拜拜嗎？

6. What are the special holidays of your religion？
   你的宗教有什麼特別節日？

7. How do you celebrate your religious holidays？
   宗教節慶時你們如何慶祝呢？

8. Does your religion dictate any dietary restrictions？
   你的宗教信仰有任何飲食方面的規定嗎？

9. Have you been exposed to other religions？
   你曾接觸過其他宗教嗎？

10. Do you believe in God？你相信上帝嗎？

11. Does your religion require any special practices？
    你的宗教信仰要求特別的教規儀式嗎？

📞 *打電話和老師討論問題*

Dialogue 1

老師：Are you a religious person ?
你信仰宗敎虔誠嗎？

學生：I don't consider myself to be very religious.
我並不認爲自己很虔誠。
➔ religious〔rɪ'lɪdʒəs〕*adj.* 信奉宗敎的；虔誠的

老師：What is your religion ?
你信仰什麼宗敎？

學生：I believe in a mixture of religions. I'm mostly Buddhist,
but I also believe in some Taoist teachings.
我是混著信的。大體而言，我是佛敎徒，但我也相信一些道敎的敎義。
➔ Buddhist〔'budɪst〕*n.* 佛敎徒　teachings〔'titʃɪŋz〕*n. pl.* 敎訓；敎旨

老師：Why do you follow your religion ?
你爲何信仰這個宗敎？

學生：I suppose it's because my parents do. I've followed
my family's religion all my life.
我想是因爲我父母也信仰這個宗敎。活到這麼大，我都跟隨著家人的
信仰。

Dialogue 2

老師：Do you attend religious services often ?
你常參加宗敎儀式嗎？

學生：No. Instead of going to the temple for services, my
family prays at the altar in our house.
不，我們家不到廟裏參加儀式，而是在家裡的神壇前拜拜。
➔ altar〔'ɔltə〕*n.* 祭壇；神壇

老師： Do you pray often?

你常拜拜嗎?

學生： Not very often. I pray only a few times each year, on religious holidays.

不常。只有每年幾次的節慶時才會拜拜。

老師： What are the special holidays of your religion?

你的宗教有那些特別的節日呢?

學生： There are several, including Chinese New Year, Lantern Festival, Tomb-Sweeping Day, Dragon Boat Festival, and Mid-Autumn Festival.

有一些啦!像是春節、元宵節、清明節、端午節和中秋節。

Dialogue 3

老師： How do you celebrate your religious holidays?

宗教節慶時,你們都如何慶祝呢?

學生： On most holidays, we pray at the family altar and burn incense. On Tomb-Sweeping Day, we go to the cemetery to pray to our ancestors, sweep their graves, burn ghost money and offer food to them.

大部分節日,我們都在家中的神壇前拜拜燒香。清明節時,我們會到墓園祭拜祖先,給祖先掃墓、燒冥紙以及擺供品。

**

lantern ('læntən) *n.* 燈籠　　festival ('fɛstəvl̩) *n.* 節日
tomb (tum) *n.* 墳墓　　incense ('ɪnsɛns) *n.* 供神所焚的香
cemetery ('sɛmə,tɛrɪ) *n.* 墓地　　ancestor ('ænsɛstə) *n.* 祖先
grave (grev) *n.* 墳墓

老師： Does your religion dictate any dietary restrictions？
你的宗教有任何飲食方面的規定嗎？

學生： Serious Buddhists are strict vegetarians, but I'm not. However, on the first and fifteenth days of each month, as well as certain holidays, most Buddhists don't eat meat.
眞正的佛敎徒是吃全素，但我不是。然而，每個月初一及十五，還有些特定節日時，大部分佛敎徒都不吃葷。

老師： Have you been exposed to other religions？
你有接觸過其他宗敎嗎？

學生： Yes. When I traveled to Europe, I visited many Catholic churches. I even attended Sunday Mass at an Italian church. I thought it was very interesting.
有。到歐洲旅遊時，我參觀了很多天主敎堂。我甚至參加了一個義大利敎堂的主日彌撒，我認爲非常有趣。

**

dictate（ˈdɪktet）v. 指定；命令　　dietary（ˈdaɪəˌtɛrɪ）adj. 有關飲食的
vegetarian（ˌvɛdʒəˈtɛrɪən）n. 素食者　　Catholic（ˈkæθəlɪk）adj. 天主敎的
Mass（mæs）n.（天主敎的）彌撒

宗敎類別

Taoism（ˈtauɪzəm，ˈdauɪzəm） 道敎　　Taoist（ˈtauɪst，ˈdauɪst） 道敎徒
Lamaism（ˈlaməɪzəm） 喇嘛敎　　Lamaist（ˈlaməɪst） 喇嘛敎徒
Buddhism（ˈbudɪzəm） 佛敎　　Buddhist（ˈbudɪst） 佛敎徒
Shintoism（ˈʃɪntoɪzm̩） 日本神道敎　　Shintoist（ˈʃɪntoɪst）. 神道敎徒
Caodaism（ˈkauˈdaɪɪzm̩） 越南高台敎　　Caodaist（ˈkauˈdaɪɪst） 高台敎徒

Hinduism（'hɪndu͵ɪzəm）印度教　　Hindu（'hɪndu）印度教徒
Brahamanism（'bramən͵ɪzəm）婆羅門教
Brahamanist（'bramənɪst）婆羅門教徒
Sikhism（'sikɪzm̩）印度錫克教　　　　Sikh〔sik〕錫克教徒
Zoroastrianism〔͵zoro'æstrɪən͵ɪzm̩）祆教；拜火教
Zoroastrian〔͵zoro'æstrɪən）祆教徒
Bahaism〔bə'haɪzm̩〕波斯泛神教　　Bahaist〔bə'haɪst〕泛神教徒
Moslemism（'mazləmɪzm̩）回教　　Moslem（'mazləm）回教徒
Islam（'ɪsləm）伊斯蘭教；伊斯蘭教徒（即回教）

❖　❖　❖　❖　❖

Judaism（'dʒudɪ͵ɪzəm）猶太教　　　　Judaist（'dʒudɪɪst）猶太教徒
Orthodox　Church 東方正教；希臘正教
Catholicism〔kə'θalə͵sɪzəm）天主教
Catholic（'kæθəlɪk）　天主教徒
Christianity〔͵krɪstʃɪ'ænətɪ, krɪs'tʃænətɪ）基督教
Christian（'krɪstʃən）基督教徒
Protestantism（'pratɪstənt͵ɪzm̩）基督新教
Protestant（'pratɪstənt）新教徒
Puritanism（'pjurətn̩͵ɪzəm）清教　　Puritan（'pjurətn̩）清教徒
Anglicanism（'æŋglɪkənɪzm̩）'，Anglican　Church 英國國教
Anglican（'æŋglɪkən）英國國教徒
Mormonism（'mɔrmənɪzm̩）摩門教　　Mormon（'mɔrmən）摩門教徒

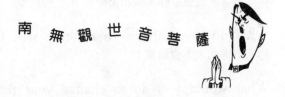

南　無　觀　世　音　菩　薩

34. Fortune Telling 算命

📞 *打電話問老師問題*

1. Have you ever been to a fortune teller?
   你算過命嗎?

2. Do you pay attention to your horoscope?
   你注意自己的星座嗎?

3. What's your sign? 你是什麼星座?

4. Can you foretell the future?
   你能預測未來嗎?

5. Do you know anyone who can tell your future?
   你認識能預知未來的人嗎?

6. Do you believe in lucky charms?
   你相信幸運物嗎?

7. Did you ever want to have your future told?
   你曾經想探詢你的未來嗎?

8. Can you tell me of different ways to look into the future, and to do fortune telling?
   你能告訴我幾個探知未來和算命的不同方法嗎?

9. What do you believe your future will be like?
   你相信你的未來會如何?

10. What would you do to change your future?
    你會如何改變你的未來?

打電話和老師討論問題

Dialogue 1

老師：Have you ever been to a fortune teller?
你去算過命嗎?

學生：Yes. I was on vacation in Europe, and I went to a carnival. There was an old Gypsy lady who did some fortune telling, and I *had my fortune told*.
有。我在歐洲度假時,參加了一個嘉年華會,有一位吉普賽老婦人會算命,我就讓她算算我的命運。

She said that I had a good future, but I doubt if she was for real.
她說我有個美好的將來,但我懷疑她是否說真話。

老師：Do you pay attention to your horoscope?
你注意自己的星座嗎?

學生：Only when I get bored. When I read the newspapers and get to the horoscopes, I normally look at mine just for recreation.
只有在我無聊的時候。在看報紙的時候讀到星座部分,我會看看自己的,當作消遣。

If it says something good, I am happy and if it says something bad, I dismiss it as rubbish!
如果說到好的事情,我會很高興,若是不好的事,我會當那是胡扯,把它忘記。

---

carnival (ˈkɑrnəvl̩) n. 嘉年華會
horoscope (ˈhɔrəˌskop, ˈhɑr-) n. 星座
dismiss (dɪsˈmɪs) v. 忘掉　　rubbish (ˈrʌbɪʃ) n. 胡說

老師：Can you foretell the future？
　　　你能預測未來嗎？

學生：In a sense, yes. It's logical really. You can work out
　　　how a lot of things will turn out if you consider all
　　　the known factors. There are some things which you
　　　can predict, but there are always things which you
　　　can never predict.
　　　在某種意義上是可以的，那真的合乎邏輯。如果你細想所有已知的
　　　事實，你就可以算出很多事情的結果。有些事情你可以預測，但永
　　　遠有你無法預知的事情。
　　　➜ foretell (for'tɛl) v. 預測　　logical ('lɑdʒɪkl̩) adj. 合邏輯的

Dialogue 2

老師：Did you ever want to have your future told？
　　　你曾經想探詢你的未來嗎？

學生：There are occasions when I wish that someone would
　　　tell me my future, but I still prefer to find out by
　　　myself. It's more exciting that way, don't you think？
　　　有些時候我會希望別人告訴我的未來會如何，但我還是比較喜歡自
　　　己去找尋答案。那樣比較刺激，你不覺得嗎？

老師：Do you believe in lucky charms？
　　　你相信幸運物嗎？

學生：I don't really, but I have some. My Austrian friend
　　　sent me a rabbit's foot as a birthday present, and I
　　　have it in my car. It's more of a decoration than a
　　　lucky charm to me.
　　　不怎麼相信，但是我有一些。我一個奧地利的朋友送給我一個兔腳
　　　當生日禮物，我把它放在車上。對我而言，它比較像是裝飾品而不
　　　是幸運物。
　　　➜ charm (tʃɑrm) n. 護符　　decoration (ˌdɛkə'reʃən) n. 裝飾品

老師：Do you know anyone who can tell you the future?
你認識能預知未來的人嗎?

學生：Not to any degree of accuracy. I normally consult the advice of my friends or family members if I am ever in doubt. I take their advice, but I don't believe that someone can come along and tell me exactly what will happen to me tomorrow.
一點都不準。若有疑惑，我通常請教朋友或家人。我接受他們的建議，但我不相信有人能跟著我，並真的告訴我明天會發生什麼事。

➡ accuracy (ˋækjərəsɪ) *n.* 正確　consult (kənˋsʌlt) *v.* 請教

Dialogue 3

老師：Can you tell me of different ways to look into the future, and to do fortune telling?
你能告訴我幾個探知未來和算命的不同方法嗎?

學生：There are many ways. Astrology looks at the stars in the sky. Oneiromancy interprets dreams as an indicator of the future.
有很多方法。占星術觀看天空中的星星；夢卜解釋夢境，作為未來的指示。

➡ astrology (əˋstralədʒɪ) *n.* 占星術
oneiromancy (oˋnaɪrə,mænsɪ) *n.* 夢卜　interpret (ɪnˋtɝprɪt) *v.* 解釋
indicator (ˋɪndə,ketɚ) *n.* 指示物

老師：What would you do to change your future?
你會如何來改變你的未來?

學生：Everything I do now will have an effect on my future, so I need to do everything *in a positive light*.
我現在的所做所為都會影響到我的未來，所以我必須積極正確地處理每一件事。

➡ positive (ˋpazətɪv) *adj.* 確實地；積極地

老師：What do you believe your future will be like？
你相信你的未來會如何？

學生：As long as I behave well and *keep to my principles*,
I believe that I will have a good future. Of course
there is always the unpredictable luck factor, but I'm
pretty optimistic.

只要我行得正且恪守自己的原則，我相信我會有個美好的未來。當
然，總會有一些難以預料的機運因素，但我是非常樂觀的。

**──────────
principle (＇prɪnsəpl̩) n. 原則　　optimistic (ˌaptə＇mɪstɪk) adj. 樂觀的

算命的方法

divination (ˌdɪvə＇neʃən) n. 占卜
omen (＇omɪn ,＇omən) n. 徵兆
astrology (ə＇stralədʒɪ) n. 占星術
palmistry (＇pamɪstrɪ) n. 手相術
phrenology (frɛ＇nalədʒɪ) n. 骨相學

☆ ☆ ☆ ☆ ☆

botanomancy (＇batnə,mænsɪ) n. 植物占卜
cartomancy (＇kartə,mænsɪ) n. 紙牌占卜
crystal gazing 水晶球占卜　＊ crystal (＇krɪstl̩) n. 水晶
sortilege (＇sɔrtl̩ɪdʒ) n. 籤卜
rhabdomancy (＇ræbdə,mænsɪ) n. 棒卜
（用神棒探索地下水源、礦藏之占卜法）

lithomancy (ˈlɪθəˌmænsɪ) *n.* 石頭占卜
numerology (ˌnjuməˈrɑlədʒɪ) *n.* 命理學
onomancy (ˈɑnəˌmænsɪ) *n.* 姓名占卜
oneiromancy (oˈnaɪrəˌmænsɪ) *n.* 夢卜
geomancy (ˈdʒiəˌmænsɪ) *n.* 土占

☆ ☆ ☆ ☆ ☆ ☆ ☆ ☆

☆ 星星王子 ☆

Capricorn (ˈkæprɪˌkɔrn) 魔羯座；山羊座 《 12 / 22 ~ 1 / 19 》

Aquarius (əˈkwɛrɪəs) 水瓶座 《 1 / 20 ~ 2 / 18 》

Pisces (ˈpaɪsiz) 雙魚座 《 2 / 19 ~ 3 / 20 》

Aries (ˈɛriz) 牡羊座 《 3 / 21 ~ 4 / 19 》

Taurus (ˈtɔrəs) 金牛座 《 4 / 20 ~ 5 / 20 》

Gemini (ˈdʒɛməˌnaɪ) 雙子座 《 5 / 21 ~ 6 / 21 》

Cancer (ˈkænsɚ) 巨蟹座 《 6 / 22 ~ 7 / 22 》

Leo (ˈlio) 獅子座 《 7 / 23 ~ 8 / 22 》

Virgo (ˈvɝgo) 處女座 《 8 / 23 ~ 9 / 22 》

Libra (ˈlɪbrə) 天秤座 《 9 / 23 ~ 10 / 23 》

Scorpio (ˈskɔrpɪˌo) 天蠍座 《 10 / 24 ~ 11 / 22 》

Sagittarius (ˌsædʒɪˈtɛrɪəs) 射手座 《 11/23 ~ 12 / 21 》

32. *Superstition* 迷 信

📞 *打電話問老師問題*

1. Are you superstitious？ 你會迷信嗎？

2. What do you think it is that makes people superstitious？
   你認為使人們迷信的原因是什麼？

3. In what ways are you superstitious？
   你在那些方面是很迷信的？

4. Have you had any weird moments in your life associated with superstition？
   在你的一生中，有過任何與迷信有關的奇特經歷嗎？

5. Were you hurt at all in the weird experience？
   你在那次奇特的經驗中有受傷嗎？

6. Do you know why 13 is regarded as such an unlucky number？ 你知道為什麼十三會被認為是個不吉利的數字？

7. Are any of your friends superstitious？
   你有朋友十分迷信嗎？

8. Do you carry lucky charms on you？
   你身上有帶幸運物嗎？

9. Do you think your beliefs will ever change in the future？
   你認為你的想法以後會改變嗎？

10. Did you learn any superstitions from your family？
    你曾從家人那裏學到任何的迷信嗎？

📞 *打電話和老師討論問題*

Dialogue 1

老師： Are you superstitious?
你迷信嗎？

學生： I would like to say that I am not, but sometimes I am. To desire an explanation for the supernatural is only human.
我想說我不迷信，但有時候也免不了會有一點。這就是人性，會想去尋求超自然現象的解釋。

老師： What do you think it is that makes people superstitious?
你認為使人們迷信的原因是什麼？

學生： I think a major factor is that people are always curious about the unknown. This is why they turn to things such as religion and superstition.
我認為主要的因素在於，人總是會對未知的事物感到好奇，所以才會去相信宗教或迷信。

老師： In what ways are you superstitious?
你在那方面會迷信？

學生： I don't blindly follow every superstitious saying; I don't wear a rabbit's foot or anything like that. Although I tend not to walk under ladders, I think that is as much common sense as superstition.
我不會盲目相信迷信的說法；我不會在身上佩戴兔子的腳或類似的東西。我刻意不從梯子下面經過，雖然這是迷信，但也是一般的常識。

**

superstitious〔ˌsupɚ'stɪʃəs〕*adj.* 迷信的
the supernatural 超自然現象

Dialogue 2

老師： Have you had any weird moments in your life associated with superstition ?

你這一生中，曾有過任何與迷信有關的奇特經驗嗎？

學生： Actually I have. It was Friday the 13th a while ago. I don't usually believe in that, but I was walking down the street past a construction site, when a rope with a metal weight on the end of it whizzed by me.

事實上，我曾經有過。時間是前一陣子十三號星期五的時候。我並不真的相信這種說法，但是當我走在街上，經過一個建築工地時，有條末端綁著金屬重物的繩子，突然從我身邊飛過。

老師： Were you hurt at all ?

你有沒有受傷呢？

學生： No! It missed my head by about 6 inches. I felt the wind of that rope cut across my face, but I was OK. I was a very lucky guy. I had no idea where that rope had come from! All the workers on duty were in awe, too.

沒有，和我的頭只差了大約六吋。我可以感覺到繩子所帶動的風吹過我的臉，但我沒什麼事。我是個非常幸運的人。我完全不知道那條繩子到底是那來的，所以有正在工作的工人也都嚇了一跳。

**

weird〔wɪrd〕*adj.* 奇異的　　*construction site* 工地
weight〔wet〕*n.* 重物　　whiz〔hwɪz〕*v.* 作颼颼聲飛馳而過
awe〔ɔ〕*n.* 驚訝

老師： Do you know why 13 is regarded as such an unlucky number ?

你知道為什麼十三會被認為是個不吉利的數字嗎？

學生： One of the reasons I know is that Jesus had 12 disciples and so 13 is unlucky; there are more, but I don't know them. Ever since the incident with the rope, I've looked at the number 13 *in a different light*.

我知道其中的一個理由是，耶穌有十二個門徒，所以十三是不吉利的；還有很多其他我不知道的理由。在這次繩子事件之後，我對於數字十三的看法又不同了。

→ disciple (dɪ'saɪpl̩) *n.* 門徒　　incident ('ɪnsədənt) *n.* 事件

Dialogue 3

老師： Are any of your friends superstitious ?

你的朋友中，有人迷信嗎？

學生： Not many of them are, but some of my friends carry with them sacred pieces of paper from temples which are said to possess positive energies. You know, so that they will protect the owner.

沒有很多，但是我有些朋友會隨身帶著從廟裡求來的符，據說是很靈驗的，你知道的，這樣可以保護隨身帶符的人。

→ sacred ('sekrɪd) *adj.* 神聖的；宗教的　　temple ('tɛmpl̩) *n.* 廟
possess (pə'zɛs) *v.* 具有

老師： Do you carry such items on you ?

你身上有帶這種東西嗎？

學生： Not personally. I don't see how a piece of paper can save me from getting mugged on my way home. But then again there are always things you don't know.

我自己沒有。我不認為一張紙就能讓我回家時不會被搶。但是總有些事是我們無法理解的。

→ mug (mʌg) *v.* 自背後襲擊、勒住脖子搶奪

老師：Do you think your beliefs will ever change in the
future ?

你認爲你的想法以後會改變嗎？

學生：I don't think so, unless something dramatic happens in
my life. One can never anticipate fully what life has
in store for him, so until that happens I think I will
remain the way I am!

我不這麼認爲，除非有十分戲劇性的事情發生在我身上。誰也不知道
自己以後會遇到什麼事，所以在那之前，我想我的想法會和現在一樣。

** ───────────

dramatic (drə'mætɪk) *adj.* 戲劇的　　anticipate (æn'tɪsə,pet) *v.* 預料
in store 必將來到或發生

心得筆記欄

33. Ghost 鬼話連篇

📞 *打電話問老師問題*

1. Do you believe that ghosts exist? 你相信有鬼嗎？

2. Have you ever seen a ghost? 你見過鬼嗎？

3. Are you afraid of ghosts? 你怕不怕鬼？

4. Where do you think ghosts come from? 你認爲鬼是那來的？

5. Do you think ghosts are evil? 你認爲鬼是邪惡的嗎？

6. What would you do if you saw a ghost?
   如果你見到鬼，你會怎麼辦？

7. Do you think ghosts only come out at night?
   你認爲鬼只有在晚上才會出現嗎？

8. Do you think there are special places where ghosts stay?
   你認爲某些特定的地方才會有鬼嗎？

9. Have any of your friends or family ever seen a ghost?
   你的朋友或家人，有人見過鬼嗎？

10. What do you think ghosts look like?
    你認爲鬼長什麼樣子？

11. Do you know any ghost stories? 你知道任何的鬼故事嗎？

12. Do you know how to get rid of ghosts?
    你知道如何驅鬼嗎？

📞 *打電話和老師討論問題*

Dialogue 1

老師： Do you believe that ghosts exist ?
　　　 你相信有鬼嗎？

學生： Yes. I certainly believe ghosts exist. So many people
　　　 have seen ghosts.
　　　 相信，我當然相信鬼是存在的。許多人都看過鬼。

老師： Have you ever seen a ghost ?
　　　 你見過鬼嗎？

學生： No, but my brother has. There was one in his dormitory
　　　 at his university. All the students who lived on his floor
　　　 saw the ghost.
　　　 沒有，不過我哥哥見過。在他大學宿舍裡就有一個。所有住在同一層
　　　 的學生都見過。

老師： What did the ghost look like ?
　　　 那個鬼長什麼樣子？

學生： My brother said she was a woman. She had long hair
　　　 and wore a long white dress.
　　　 我哥哥說她是個女鬼。頭髮長長的，身穿白色的衣服。

Dialogue 2

老師： Are you afraid of ghosts ?
　　　 你怕不怕鬼？

學生： Yes. I don't even like to think about ghosts because
　　　 they scare me so much.
　　　 怕啊。我甚至連想都不敢想，因為我真的很怕鬼。

老師：Where do you think ghosts come from？
你認為鬼是那來的？

學生：I think ghosts are the spirits of people who didn't die naturally. Their spirits are troubled because they died too early.
我認為鬼是那些死於非命者的靈魂。他們的靈魂覺得十分困擾，因為他們死得太早了。

老師：Do you think ghosts are evil？
你認為鬼很邪惡嗎？

學生：No. I don't think they're evil, but I'm still frightened of them. I think ghosts are probably more lonely than evil.
不，我不認為他們很邪惡，但是我還是很怕鬼。我認為鬼是寂寞而非邪惡。

Dialogue 3

老師：What would you do if you saw a ghost？
如果你看見鬼，你會怎麼辦？

學生：I'd be very frightened. I'd probably run away as quickly as possible.
我會很害怕，而且可能會儘快跑掉。

老師：Do you think ghosts come out only at night？
你認為鬼在晚上才會出現嗎？

學生：No, I think ghosts can come out at any time of the day. Maybe people see ghosts more at night because it's quiet and dark.
不，我認為鬼在一天中的任何時間都會出現。也許人們較常在晚上見鬼，因為晚上比較安靜而且比較暗。

老師： Do you think there are special places where ghosts stay？
你認爲某些特定的地方才有鬼嗎？

學生： I think ghosts probably haunt certain places, such as
cemeteries, the places where they died, and where they
once lived.
我認爲在某些地方才會鬧鬼，像是墓地、他們死去的地方，以及他們
生前住過的地方。

老師： Do you know how to get rid of ghosts？
你知道如何驅鬼嗎？

學生： Not really. But I heard that saying some incantations
and ignoring the provocation of ghosts will protect
you from harm.
不是很清楚。不過我聽說念些咒語，並且不要理會鬼的挑釁，就可以
安然無恙。

**

haunt (hɔnt) *v.* （鬼魂）出沒   cemetery (ˈsɛmə,tɛrɪ) *n.* 墓地
incantation (ˌɪnkænˈteʃən) *n.* 咒語   provocation (ˌprɑvəˈkeʃən) *n.* 挑釁

34. Credit Card 信用卡

📞 *打電話問老師問題*

1. Do you have a credit card？ 你有信用卡嗎？

2. How often do you use a credit card？
   你多久使用一次信用卡？

3. When do you usually use a credit card？
   你通常什麼時候使用信用卡？

4. What type of credit cards do you have？
   你的信用卡是那一種？

5. Does your credit card company offer you special incentives to use its card？
   你的發卡公司有提供用卡優惠嗎？

6. Have you ever had trouble with your credit card？
   你使用信用卡有遇過什麼困難嗎？

7. Do you believe credit cards can be financially dangerous？
   你認為信用卡會造成財務危機嗎？

8. What do you think are the positive aspects of using credit cards？ 你認為使用信用卡有何正面意義？

9. What do you think are the negative aspects of using credit cards？ 你認為使用信用卡有何負面意義？

📞 *打電話和老師討論問題*

Dialogue 1

老師：Do you have a credit card?
你有信用卡嗎？

學生：Actually, I have two credit cards.
事實上，我有兩張信用卡。

老師：How often do you use a credit card?
你多久使用一次信用卡？

學生：I use my credit cards a few times per week, and usually not more than ten times per month.
每個禮拜使用幾次，通常一個月不超過十次。

老師：When do you usually use a credit card?
你通常什麼時候使用信用卡？

學生：I usually use my credit cards when I buy something relatively expensive, such as clothing or meals at nice restaurants. I do not use my credit cards for everyday purchases, such as groceries.
買比較貴的物品時，像是衣服或是在高級餐廳吃飯時，我通常會使用信用卡。我不會用信用卡買雜貨類等日常用品。

**

purchase (ˈpɝtʃəs) *n.* 購買　　grocery (ˈgrosərɪ) *n.* 雜貨

Dialogue 2

老師： What type of credit cards do you have？
你的信用卡是那一種？

學生： I have a Visa card and an American Express Card.
我有一張 Visa 卡和一張美國運通卡。

老師： Does your credit card company offer you special incentives to use its card？
你的發卡公司提供用卡的優惠嗎？

學生： Yes. Visa offers me five airline frequent flier miles every one thousand dollars I charge on its card. American Express offers me points which can be used to obtain free gifts.
有的。用 Visa 簽帳，每一千元就可獲得免費搭乘航空公司班機五英哩的優待。美國運通卡是積點數換取贈品。

老師： Have you ever had trouble with your credit card？
你使用信用卡有遭遇過麻煩嗎？

學生： Last year, I was charged twice for a purchase on my Visa card. But, once I pointed out the error, Visa immediately corrected it.
去年有一次我用 Visa 卡買東西，但卻要繳二次費用。經我一指出錯誤，Visa 立刻改正過來。

**─────────────────

incentive〔ɪnˋsɛntɪv〕*n.* 鼓勵；刺激

Dialogue 3

老師： Do you believe credit cards can be financially dangerous ?
你認為信用卡會造成財務危機嗎？

學生： Yes. I have a friend who cannot control his credit card use. Now he has *a large debt to pay off*.
會。我有一個朋友，使用信用卡不知節制，現在，他有一大筆債務要償還。

老師： What do you think are the positive aspects of using a credit card ?
你認為使用信用卡有什麼正面意義？

學生： I think credit cards are very convenient to use. I also like receiving statements that show me how I spend my money each month.
我認為使用信用卡非常方便，而且，我喜歡收帳單來了解我每個月的開銷。

老師： What do you think are the negative aspects of using a credit card ?
你認為使用信用卡有什麼負面影響？

學生： I think credit cards can make it too easy to spend money. People have to be careful when they use their credit cards.
我認為使用信用卡很容易就把錢花掉。使用信用卡消費時，應該要小心。

**

debt〔dɛt〕*n.* 負債　　***pay off*** 償還
positive〔'pɑzətɪv〕*adj.* 正面的；積極的　　aspect〔'æspɛkt〕*n.* 方面
statement〔'stetmənt〕*n.* 帳目　　negative〔'nɛgətɪv〕*adj.* 否定的

35. *Computer* 電 腦

📞 *打電話問老師問題*

1. Do you know how to use a computer?
   你知道如何使用電腦嗎?

2. Do you own a computer? 你有電腦嗎?

3. What model of computer do you have?
   你的電腦是那種機型?

4. What are the specifications of your computer?
   你的電腦有什麼特色?

5. What programs are you familiar with? 你會那些軟體?

6. Do you ever use e-mail? 你使用過電子郵件嗎?

7. Do you use computers in college?
   你在學校裡使用電腦嗎?

8. Does your computer have fax capability?
   你的電腦有傳真功能嗎?

9. Is your computer as powerful as you want?
   你的電腦功能是你所想要的嗎?

10. What do you think the future of computers will be?
    你認為電腦的前景如何?

11. Do you have plans to upgrade your computer?
    你有計畫要昇級你的電腦嗎?

📞 打電話和老師討論問題

Dialogue 1

老師：Do you know how to use a computer?
你知道如何使用電腦嗎?

學生：Not very well, but I know enough about it to do what I want to do. Actually, I only use it for very basic applications such as word processing.
不是很在行,不過足夠應付我所要處理的事情。事實上,我都使用電腦來執行一些很基本的應用軟體,像是文書處理之類。

老師：Do you own a computer?
你有電腦嗎?

學生：I have a Pentium 75. It was the state of the art computer when it *came out*, but these days it's considered an "old" machine to hackers. I'm very satisfied with what it can do, though.
我有台娉婷 75,它剛上市的時候算是電腦中的極品,但是,現在已被玩家認為是「老舊」的機型。不過,我對它的功能感到很滿意。

老師：What programs are you *familiar with*?
你會那些軟體?

學生：I've used the Windows versions of Microsoft Office. I think the program that I use the most often is Word 6.0. I use it just about every day.
我使用過視窗環境下的微軟辦公室系統。我想我最常用的程式是 Word 6.0 版,我幾乎每天使用。

** ─────────────

application (ˌæpləˈkeʃən) *n.* 應用之物　*come out* 出版;發售
hacker (ˈhækɚ) *n.* 電腦玩家

Dialogue 2

老師 : Do you ever use e-mail?
你使用過電子郵件嗎?

學生 : Of course! I have some friends abroad and at other universities in Taiwan, so I use the e-mail system to *keep in touch*. It's very convenient.
當然!我有一些朋友在國外,以及台灣其他的大學裡,我利用電子郵件和他們保持聯繫,相當地方便。

老師 : Do you use computers at college?
你在學校裡使用電腦嗎?

學生 : Yes. I normally use them for *academic purposes,* but when I get the time, I use them to *access the net*.
是的,我大多因課業需要而使用電腦。不過,當我有空閒時,就利用它們來連上網路。

老師 : What are the specifications of your computer?
你的電腦有什麼特色?

學生 : It's a Pentium 75. At the moment I have 8 megs of RAM and a 540 meg Hard disk. I'm planning on upgrading it to 16 megs of RAM and one gigabyte of Hard disk. I had a P-60, but it had the famous Pentium bug, so I upgraded it to a P-75.
我的電腦是娉婷 75,目前配有 8MB 的記憶體和 540MB 的硬碟。我打算把它昇級到 16MB 的記憶體和 1GB 容量的硬碟。我原本使用 P-60 的中央處理器,不過它是出了名的有問題,所以我就把它換成 P-75。

**　****

keep in touch 保持聯繫
academic〔͵ækə'dɛmɪk〕*adj.* 學術的
Pentium〔'pɛntɪəm〕英代爾公司所生產的 586 CPU

Dialogue 3

老師： Does your computer have fax capability ?
你的電腦有傳眞功能嗎？

學生： Of course! I bought a fax modem last week. It's *hooked up* to the computer, and now I am able to use the net as well as having fax capability.
當然！我上個星期買了台有傳眞功能的數據機，我將它接在電腦上，這樣我不但能連上網路，還能當傳眞機呢。

老師： Is your computer as powerful as you want ?
你電腦的功能是你所想要的嗎？

學生： No. As I've said, the CPU is quite powerful, but I need the extra RAM to maximize my computer's potential. All the new programs these days need extra RAM to run smoothly.
不，正如我所說的，它的中央處理器相當有力，但是我需要更多的記憶體來增強電腦的潛力。現在的新軟體需要較多的記憶體，執行起來才能順暢。

老師： What do you think the future of computers will be ?
你認爲電腦的前景如何？

學生： I think everyone will have their own computers in the future. I think that computers will *take over* the simpler things in life such as paying your bills, allowing us to do more of what we want to do.
我想在未來，每個人都將擁有自己的電腦。我認爲電腦會接管生活中一些簡單的事務，像是繳費啦，讓我們做更多想做的事。

** ───────────────

capability (ˌkepəˋbɪlətɪ) *n.* 能力　　modem (ˋmodm̩) *n.* 數據機
hook up 接裝　　maximize (ˋmæksəˌmaɪz) *v.* 增加至極限
potential (pəˋtɛnʃəl) *n.* 潛力　　*take over* 接管

電腦教室

電腦的資料單位

bit〔bɪt〕　電腦最基本的資料單位
byte〔baɪt〕　1 byte = 8 bits
1KB (kilobytes) = 1024 bytes
1MB (megabytes) = 1024　KB = 1,048,576 bytes
1GB (gigabytes) = 1024　MB = 1,073,741,824 bytes

電腦的零件與周邊

CPU = Central　Processing　Unit　中央處理器
RAM = Random　Access　Memory　隨機存取記憶體
ROM = Read　Only　Memory　唯讀記憶體
mother　board　主機板　　　　　　keyboard　鍵盤
mouse　滑鼠　　　　　　　　　　monitor〔'manətɚ〕顯示器
floppy　disk　軟碟　　　　　　　hard　disk　硬碟
CD-ROM　drive　唯讀光碟機
MO (= Magneto　Optical) 可讀寫式光碟機
＊magneto〔mæg'nito〕*n.* 久磁發電機　＊optical〔'ɑptɪkl〕*adj.* 光學式
printer　印表機　　　　　　　　　modem〔'modm̩〕　數據機

常見電腦名詞簡介

♣ DOS (Disk　Operating　System) 『磁碟作業系統』
　個人電腦上常見的個人用作業系統，有 MS-DOS ， PC-DOS 等等。

♣ INTEL 『英代爾』
　為一家設計、製造生產半導體、微處理器之國際性公司， PC 上的 CPU
　(如 486 、 Pentium) 即為 Intel 之代表作。

♣ IBM (International Business Machine Corp.,) 『國際商務機器公司』
　很多有名的電腦系統即為 IBM 所設計製造，如 AS/400 ， PS/2 等等。

♣ MACINTOSH 『麥金塔』

簡稱 Mac，是蘋果電腦公司的電腦代表作，其使用上之親和力十分著名。蘋果電腦公司另有一新作，為 PowerMac，是使用新一代的『威力晶片』PowerPC 當 CPU。

♣ MICROSOFT 『微軟』

一家十分著名的軟體公司。從早先的 MS-DOS、MS-Windows，至各式各樣的 Windows 軟體，如 Word、Excel、PowerPoint、PageMaker 等等，均為 Microsoft 之作品。

♣ PENTIUM

Intel 目前在 PC 的 CPU 市場上之主力產品，執行速度十分快速，預計 96 年度 CPU 市場應為 Pentium 之天下（486 將退出主力，甚至淘汰）。

♣ OS/2

IBM 所推出之 32 位元作業系統，早先僅能在 IBM 之 PS/2 個人電腦上執行，但因應市場需要，已改進為一般相容 PC 也能執行。目前最新的版本是 OS/2 3.0（Warp），為 Windows 95 之最大對手。

♣ WINDOWS

微軟公司所推出的作業系統，目前常見的版本為較舊的 Windows 3.1、Windows NT，及新推出的 Windows 95。

♣ UNIX

多人多工的標準作業系統，提供了完整的網路環境（包括了 TCP/IP，使用 Internet），及程式寫作環境，常用於工作站級以上的電腦。

♣ LINUX

一套免費的 Unix 作業系統，最早由芬蘭赫爾辛基大學學生，Linus 所開發，後由世界各地熱心之程式設計者及學生合作撰寫。現不但適用於個人電腦，另也在其他平台上陸續開發。目前的主要使用者為學生，尤其是資訊相關科系者。而因其系統及原始程式均免費，漸漸也有公司看上這套作業系統，使用它來提供 Internet（如 WWW，FTP）之相關服務。

36. *Internet* 網際網路

📞 *打電話問老師問題*

1. Have you heard of the Internet? 你聽過網際網路嗎?

2. What exactly is the Internet? 網際網路到底是什麼?

3. What does the Internet consist of? 網際網路如何組成?

4. What type of people use the Internet?
   什麼樣的人在使用網際網路?

5. What kind of information can I obtain on the Internet?
   我能從網際網路上得到什麼樣的資訊?

6. What is the most common use of the Internet?
   網際網路最普遍的用途是什麼?

7. How can I access the Internet?
   我要如何連上網際網路?

8. Is there anything else I need to know about the Internet?
   關於網際網路,還有什麼我需要知道呢?

9. What other features of the Internet are there apart from
   e-mail? 除了電子郵件之外,網際網路還有那些特色?

10. How many people in the world access the Internet?
    全球有多少人連上網際網路?

11. What's the future of the Internet?
    網際網路的前景如何?

📞 *打電話和老師討論問題*

Dialogue 1

老師： Have you heard of the Internet?
你聽過網際網路嗎？

學生： Of course. Actually I already have an account and my
own homepage.
當然。事實上我已經有帳號還有自己的介紹首頁。

老師： What exactly is the Internet?
網際網路到底是什麼？

學生： It was first devised by the American military as a means
of communications between important bases *in the event
of* nuclear warfare. But over the years it has evolved
into a more conventional information system.
網際網路最早是由美國軍方所發展，作爲核子戰爭時，重要基地之間
的通訊工具。不過這些年來，它已演變爲一相當普遍的資訊系統。

老師： What does the Internet consist of?
網際網路如何組成？

學生： It is essentially a system which consists of millions of
computer nodes linked by satellite and telephone lines
worldwide. Each node contributes to the net by having
some sort of information which you can access.
基本上，它是利用全球的衛星與電話線，將幾百萬部像節點一樣的電
腦連結起來的系統。每一個點提供某些可供使用的資訊，貢獻資源到
網路上。

**

base (bes) *n.* 基地　　*in the event of* 在～情況之下
nuclear ('n(j)uklɪɚ) *n.* 核子　　warfare ('wɔr,fɛr) *n.* 戰爭
evolve (ɪ'valv) *v.* 演進　　conventional (kən'vɛnʃən!) *adj.* 通常的
node (nod) *n.* 點　　satellite ('sætḷ,aɪt) *n.* 衛星　　contribute (kən'trɪbjut) *v.* 貢獻

Dialogue 2

老師： What type of people use the Internet？
什麼樣的人在使用網際網路？

學生： Most of the information you have on the net is still academic, so it is very useful to students. But the number of entertainment and other multimedia communications are growing very rapidly, so more and more people use it for entertainment purposes.
網路上大部分的資訊仍屬學術性質，所以它對學生相當有用。不過娛樂方面與其他種類的多媒體通訊，正快速地成長，因此愈來愈多的人使用網際網路，作爲娛樂用途。
→ multimedia (ˌmʌltɪˈmidɪə) *n.* 多媒體

老師： What kind of information can I obtain on the Internet？ 我能從網際網路上得到什麼樣的資訊？

學生： The amount and variety of information on the net is vast. You can find anything from the latest international news to reserving a flight for your next holiday!
網路上的資訊量與種類非常多。從最新的國際新聞，到下一次假期預訂機票的服務，都可以找得到。

老師： What is the most common use of the Internet？
網際網路最普遍的用途是什麼？

學生： Most people use it for electronic mail, or e-mail. It allows users to send messages, letters, pictures and anything digital across the globe at the touch of a button. It allows you to ***keep in touch with*** more people than by writing letters.
大部分的人都使用電子郵件功能，也就是所說的 e-mail。只要觸動鍵盤，使用者便可將訊息、信件、圖片、以及任何數位的資料，傳送到地球的彼端。比起寫信來，它能使你與更多的人保持聯繫。
→ digital (ˈdɪdʒətl̩) *n.* 數位　　***keep in touch with*** *sb.* 與某人保持聯繫

Dialogue 3

老師： How can I access the Internet?
我要如何連上網際網路？

學生： You can either use a computer in your school or the one you have at home. For your home PC you will need to install a modem which will be connected to your telephone line. Then you'll need to subscribe to an Internet company for which a monthly fee is payable.
你可以使用學校或家裡的電腦。使用家裡的個人電腦，你需要安裝數據機連接電話線。然後，你必須向網路公司申請使用，繳納月費。

老師： That doesn't sound too hard. Is there anything else I'll need to know?
聽起來不會太困難。還有什麼事我需要知道嗎？

學生： *The net is free for now.* All you will need to pay is the cost of the phone call from your house to the net company that you've subscribed to.
網路資源目前是免費的，你所要負擔的就是從家裡打到網路公司的電話費。

老師： What other features of the Internet are there apart from e-mail? 除了電子郵件之外，網際網路還有那些特色？

學生： You can use IRC which allows you to talk to other users around the world, and FTP which allows you to retrieve information all over the world. *There is a lot more to the net* than just e-mail!
你可以使用線上交談，和世界各地的使用者談話，檔案傳輸協定可讓你取得全球各地的資料。除了電子郵件之外，網路上的資源可多呢！

**
***

PC = Personal Computer 個人電腦　　install〔ɪnˋstɔl〕v. 安裝
modem〔ˋmodm〕n. 數據機　　subscribe〔səbˋskraɪb〕v. 申請
FTP = file transfer protocol　　protocol〔ˋprotəˌkɑl〕n. 協定
retrieve〔rɪˋtriv〕v. 取回

Internet 上的主要工具與資源簡介

♥E-Mail，Electronic Mail『電子郵件』
運用信件處理的方式，提供網路使用者彼此傳遞訊息。

♥FTP，File Transfer Protocol『檔案傳輸協定』
一般有帳號之使用者，可與另一遠端機器以 FTP 的方法傳輸檔案；而
也有不少 FTP Server 提供 anonymous（使用者無需表示身份），抓取
免費檔案之服務。

♥Telnet『遠程終端模擬』
利用自己正在使用之電腦（帳號），連至另一台您可以 login 的電腦，
（也要有帳號使用權）使用之。

♥Remote Login『遠端上機』
使用者若有某部電腦的使用帳號，可利用手邊的電腦連上該主機，取
用其上儲存的各類資料。

♥Netnews『電子論壇』
使用者可按自己的興趣與需求，加入不同的討論群，除可接收來自全
球的新資訊，亦可發表言論或提出問題。

♥Gopher『小田鼠資料查詢系統』
選單式的查詢文數字資料服務。使用者藉著選單式界面，可以快速地
搜尋到所需的資料。

♥WWW，World Wide Web『全球超媒體資訊網』
把聲音、圖片、格式化的文章等等活潑的多媒體資訊，以人機界面和
超文字（Hypertext）方式，加入 Internet 中。現在的 WWW 上可說是
琳琅滿目，因為其資訊提供方式十分活潑，已被各行各業廣泛使用。

♥BBS，Bulletin Board System『電子佈告欄系統』
提供各類訊息的佈告。部份 BBS 亦可進行討論、線上交談、檔案存取等服務。

♥IRC，Internet Relay Chat『線上交談服務』
將電腦彼此相連，以鍵盤來作交談。鍵盤所打出來的字，會立即出現在交談者的螢幕上，馬上即可回覆。

要連上 Internet。必須向提供 Internet 連線服務的網路中心或公司申辦帳戶。台灣連通 Internet 的三大網路如下，您可參考所列資料，向其索取有關資料。

服務對象	學校及研究機構	公民營機構及一般個人	
網路名稱	TANet （台灣學術網路）	HiNet （網際資訊網路）	SEEDNET （種子網路）
負責單位	教育部 電子計算機中心	交通部 數據通信所	財團法人 資訊工業策進會
聯 絡 電 話	(02) 7377439	台北：(02) 3442790 桃園：(03) 3351644 新竹：(035) 212329 台中：(080) 400111 彰化：(080) 471123 嘉義：(05) 2444285 台南：(06) 2442250 高雄：(07) 2121040 其他：當地電信局	台北中心： (02) 7336454 (02) 7338779 新竹中心： (035) 773311 轉 518 高雄中心： (07) 3394105 其他：請擇近聯絡上列 服務中心

37. Pets & Stray Animals
寵物與流浪動物

📞 *打電話問老師問題*

1. Do you have a pet？ 你有寵物嗎？

2. What kind of animal is it？ 是那一種動物？

3. How old is your pet？ 你的寵物年紀多大？

4. Is your pet neutered？ 你的寵物結紮了嗎？

5. Is it difficult to care for your pet？
   照顧你的寵物困難嗎？

6. Have you ever thought of adopting a stray animal？
   你曾想過收養流浪動物嗎？

7. How often do you feed your pet？
   你多久餵你的寵物一次？

8. Do you take your pets to a veterinarian？
   你帶寵物去看醫生嗎？

9. Do you feel sorry for stray animals？
   你是否為流浪動物感到難過呢？

10. Do you think stray animals are dangerous？
    你覺得流浪動物危險嗎？

11. How can we solve the problem of stray animals？
    我們該如何解決流浪動物的問題？

📞 *打電話和老師討論問題*

Dialogue 1

老師：Do you have a pet ?
你有寵物嗎？

學生：Yes, I own a dog.
是的，我有一隻狗。

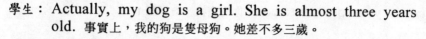

老師：How old is he ?
他年紀多大？

學生：Actually, my dog is a girl. She is almost three years
old. 事實上，我的狗是隻母狗。她差不多三歲。

老師：Has she been neutered ?
她結紮了嗎？

學生：Yes, as soon as she was old enough, I had her neutered.
I think that there are already too many stray animals
living on the streets.
是啊，她年紀夠大時，我就讓她結紮了。我覺得街道上已有太多的流
浪動物了。

老師：I agree with you. Have you ever thought of adopting
a stray animal ?
我同意。你曾想過收養流浪動物嗎？

學生：In fact, my dog was a stray animal. I found her outside
my apartment building when she was only a puppy. She
was so cute that I had to take her home with me.
事實上，我的狗就是流浪動物。當她還是幼犬時，我在我公寓外發現
她。她是如此可愛，所以我不得不帶她回家。

** ────────────────────

neuter（'njutɚ）*v.* 閹割　　adopt（ə'dɑpt）*v.* 收養　　stray（stre）*adj.* 走失的

Dialogue 2

老師： Is it difficult to take care of your dog?
照顧你的狗困難嗎？

學生： No, it's not very hard. I walk her every morning before I go to work and every evening after I come home.
不，不是很困難。每天早上上班前和每天晚上回家後，我都會帶她散步。

老師： How often do you feed her?
你多久餵她一次？

學生： I fill her bowl with dry dog food every morning. And I often give her the scraps left over from dinner.
每天早上我在她的碗裡裝滿乾狗食，而晚上常給她晚餐剩下的飯菜。

老師： Do you take her to a veterinarian?
你帶她去看獸醫嗎？

學生： Yes, I take her to the vet for annual check-ups. Of course, if she's ever sick or hurt, I take her to the vet right away.
是的，我帶她去看獸醫，做一年一度的健康檢查。當然，如果她生病或是受傷，我會馬上帶她去看獸醫。

Dialogue 3

老師： Do you feel sorry for stray animals?
你為流浪動物感到難過嗎？

學生： Yes. Every time I see a stray animal, I want to take it home and care for it.
是的，每次看到流浪動物，我都想帶牠回家並照顧牠。

** scraps (skræps) *n. pl.* 剩飯　　veterinarian (= vet) (ˌvɛtərəˈnɛrɪən) *n.* 獸醫

老師：Do you think stray animals are dangerous?
你覺得流浪動物危險嗎？

學生：They can be dangerous if they carry diseases. But I'm not afraid of them because I feel so much pity for them.
如果他們帶病的話，會很危險。但我不怕，因為我十分同情他們。

老師：How can we solve the problem of stray animals?
我們該如何解決流浪動物的問題？

學生：I think people should never abandon their pets. The government should tell people to think more carefully before they get a pet, so they don't abandon it later. And I think most pets should be neutered, so their owners don't *get stuck with* a lot of puppies or kittens.
我覺得人們不應該丟棄寵物。政府應該教導民眾，在養寵物之前，要仔細考慮，這樣以後才不會遺棄。而且我覺得大部分的寵物都應該結紮，這樣主人才不會被一大堆的小狗或小貓弄得不知所措。

**

abandon (ə'bændən) v. 丟棄　　*get stuck with* 被迫做 (討厭的事)
kitten ('kɪtn̩) n. 小貓

可愛小狗

♥ 小型狗

Beagle ('bigl̩) 米格魯　　　　　　Chihuahua (tʃɪ'wawa) 吉娃娃
Chin (tʃɪn) 狆
Japanese spitz 狐狸狗　　*spitz (spɪts) n. 長毛狗

Maltese〔mɔl'tiz〕馬爾濟斯　　Papillon〔'pæpə,lɑn〕蝴蝶狗

Pekingese〔,pikɪŋ'iz〕北京狗

Pomeranian〔,pɑmə'renɪə〕博美狗

Poodle〔'pudḷ〕貴賓狗　　　　　Pug〔pʌg〕巴哥

Schnauzer〔'ʃnauzɚ〕雪納瑞　　Shih tze 西施

Yorkshire Terrier〔'jɔrkʃɪr 'tɛrɪɚ〕約克夏狾

West Highland White Terrier 西高地白狾

♥ 中型狗

Shetland Sheepdog〔'ʃɛtlənd 'ʃipdɔg〕雪特蘭牧羊犬（喜樂蒂）

Siberian Husky〔saɪ'bɪrɪən 'hʌskɪ〕哈士奇

Shiba〔'ʃɪbə〕柴犬　　　　　　Chow Chow〔tʃau tʃau〕鬆獅犬

Dalmatian〔dæl'meʃɪən〕大麥町（卡通「101忠狗」的狗主角）

Cocker Spaniel〔'kɑkɚ 'spænjəl〕科卡

Dachshound〔'dɑks,hund〕臘腸狗

Basset Hound〔'bæsɪt 'haund〕巴吉度獵犬

Bulldog〔'bul,dɔg〕牛頭犬

Greyhound〔'gre,haund〕靈猩

Bull Terrier 牛頭狾（「家有賤狗」漫畫中的狗主角）

♥ 大型狗

Akita〔ɑ'kɪtə〕秋田

Alaska Malamute〔ə'læskə 'mælə,mjut〕愛斯基摩犬

Boxer〔'bɑksɚ〕拳師狗

Collie〔'kɑlɪ〕長毛牧羊犬（電視影集「靈犬萊西」的狗主角）

German Shepherd Dog 德國牧羊犬（狼犬）

Golden Retriever 黃金獵犬

Labrador Retriever〔'læbrə,dɔr rɪ'trivɚ〕拉布拉多導盲犬

Mastiff〔'mæstɪf〕獒犬

Rottweiler〔'rɑt,waɪlɚ〕洛威拿

St. Bernard〔sent 'bɜnɚd〕聖伯納（電影「我家也有貝多芬」的狗主角）

38. *Wildlife Conservation*
野生生物保育

📞 *打電話問老師問題*

1. Are you concerned about the survival of endangered species ? 你關心瀕臨絕種動物的生存嗎 ?

2. Do you think it is wrong to make jewelry out of elephant ivory and turtle shells ?
你是否覺得用象牙和龜殼來做珠寶是不對的呢 ?

3. Do you think it is wrong to make medicines out of tigers and other endangered species ?
你是否覺得用老虎，和其他瀕臨絕種危險的動物來製藥，是不對的呢 ?

4. Are you concerned about the preservation of the rainforests ?
你關心雨林的保存嗎 ?

5. Do you think it is wrong to clear rainforests for farming ?
你是否覺得清除雨林來耕作是不對的呢 ?

6. Do you think it is wrong to chop down trees for paper ?
你是否覺得砍下樹木來造紙是不對的呢 ?

7. Do you think pollution threatens the survival of wildlife ?
你是否覺得污染威脅了野生生物的生存 ?

8. What do you think is the most dangerous threat to wildlife ?
你覺得對野生動植物最危險的威脅是什麼 ?

9. What do you think people should do to improve wildlife conservation ? 你覺得人類應該如何來加強對野生生物的保育呢 ?

📞 *打電話和老師討論問題*

Dialogue 1

老師 : Are you concerned about the survival of endangered
　　　species ?
　　　你關心瀕臨絕種動物的生存嗎？

學生 : Yes, I am. It is sad that more and more species are
　　　becoming extinct every year. Future generations will
　　　only be able to learn about our ***endangered species***
　　　from books.
　　　是的，我關心。每年都有愈來愈多的動物絕種，眞是令人難過。未來
　　　的子孫只能從書本中得知瀕臨絕種的動物了。

老師 : Do you think it is wrong to make jewelry out of
　　　elephant ivory and turtle shells ?
　　　你是否覺得用象牙和龜殼來做珠寶是不對的？

學生 : Yes. I do. I don't think people should kill endangered
　　　species just to make jewelry; there are plenty of ways
　　　to decorate the body.
　　　是的，我是這麼認爲。我認爲人不應該只爲了要做珠寶，而殺瀕臨絕
　　　種的動物；有許多方式可以來裝飾身體。

** ―――――――――――
　　concern〔kən'sɝn〕v. 擔心　　survival〔sə'vaɪvl̩〕n. 生存
　　endangered〔ɪn'dendʒəd〕adj. 瀕臨絕種的
　　species〔'spiʃiz〕n. 種　　extinct〔ɪk'stɪŋkt〕adj. 絕種的
　　generation〔,dʒɛnə'reʃən〕n. 一代
　　jewelry〔'dʒuəlrɪ〕n. 珠寶　　*make ~ out of ~* 用~做成~
　　ivory〔'aɪvərɪ〕n. 象牙　　shell〔ʃɛl〕n. 殼
　　plenty of 很多　　decorate〔'dɛkə,ret〕v. 裝飾

老師： Do you think it is wrong to make medicines out of tigers and other endangered species ?
你是否覺得用老虎，和其他瀕臨絕種的動物來製藥，是不對的？

學生： I think medicines are important, but I believe effective medicines can be made out of materials other than endangered species.
我認為藥很重要，但是我相信，有效的藥能從瀕臨絕種動物之外的材料製成。

Dialogue 2

老師： Are you concerned about the preservation of rainforests ? 你關心雨林的保存嗎？

學生： Yes, I am. I've heard that rainforests are being destroyed *at a frightening pace*. I wish there was some way that an ordinary civilian like myself could help end this horrible situation.
是的，我關心。我聽說雨林正以驚人的速度遭到破壞。我希望有方法能讓像我這樣的平凡百姓，幫忙終止這種可怕的情形。

老師： Do you think it is wrong to clear rainforests for farming ? 你是否覺得清除雨林來耕作是不對的呢？

學生： Of course. If people really need farmland, then I think they should concern themselves with reducing their need to consume meat, since the rainforests are mostly being cleared to *make space for* grazing cattle.
當然。如果人們真的需要耕地，那麼我想他們應該去關心如何來減少對肉類的需求，因為大部分被清除的雨林，都是為放牧牛群製造空間。

** ───────

preservation (ˌprɛzɚ'veʃən) n. 保存；保護　　rainforest ('ren,fɔrɪst) n. 雨林
frightening ('fraɪtnɪŋ) adj. 令人驚嚇的　　civilian (sə'vɪljən) n. 平民
graze (grez) v. 放牧　　cattle ('kætl̩) n. 牛

老師： Do you think it is wrong to chop down trees for paper?
你是否覺得砍下樹木來造紙是不對的呢？

學生： I believe it is necessary to chop down some trees for paper, but also that people should try to recycle the paper they use as well as reforest the land.
我相信砍下一些樹木來造紙是必須的，但是人們也應試著回收廢紙並且重新造林。

Dialogue 3

老師： Do you think pollution threatens the survival of wildlife?
你是否覺得污染威脅了野生動植物的生存？

學生： Yes. I think pollution can destroy forests, oceans, and other important wildlife habitats.
是的。我覺得污染會毀滅森林、海洋，以及其他重要的野生生物棲息地。

老師： What do you think is the most dangerous threat to wildlife?
你覺得對野生動植物最危險的威脅是什麼？

學生： I think humans are the most dangerous threat to wildlife. People kill animals and plants too carelessly.
我覺得人類是對野生動植物最危險的威脅。人們過於輕率地殺害動物和植物。

＊＊
chop〔tʃɑp〕v. 劈砍　　recycle〔riˋsaɪk!〕v. 循環利用
reforest〔riˋfɔrɪst〕v. 重新造林　　threaten〔ˋθrɛtn̩〕v. 威脅
wildlife〔ˋwaɪldˏlaɪf〕n. 野生動植物
habitat〔ˋhæbəˏtæt〕n. 棲息地；生長地　　threat〔θrɛt〕n. 威脅

老師： What do you think people should do to improve wild-
life conservation？

你覺得人類應該如何來加強對野生生物的保護呢？

學生： I think people should not buy products made out of
endangered species and try not to pollute their environment. They should also ask their governments to
act to conserve wildlife.

我覺得人們不應該購買以瀕臨絕種動物所製成的產品，而且也該盡
量不要污染環境。此外，也應該要求政府採取行動來保護野生生物。

** ─────

conservation (ˌkɑnsə'veʃən) *n.* 保護；保存
conserve (kən'sɝv) *v.* 保存；保護

☆ 生態保育相關語彙

rhinoceros (raɪ'nɑsərəs) *n.* 犀牛	rhino ('raɪno) *n.* 犀牛
rhino horn 犀牛角	panda ('pændə) *n.* 熊貓
orangutan (o'ræŋuˌtæn) *n.* 紅毛猩猩	
mistreat (mɪs'trit) *v. n.* 虐待	
specimen ('spɛsəmən) *n.* 標本	stuffed animal 標本
swamp (swɑmp) *n.* 沼澤	flay (fle) *v.* 剝皮
Snake Alley 華西街 (蛇巷)	ecology (ɪ'kɑlədʒɪ) *n.* 生態
poacher ('potʃə) *n.* 盜獵者	elimination (ɪˌlɪmə'neʃən) *n.* 消失
Wildlife Conservation Law 野生動植物保育法	

sexual potency 性能力 ＊potency ('potn̩sɪ) *n.* 能力

CITES 瀕臨絕種動物國際貿易會議

(= Convention on International Trade in Endangered Species)

39. Pollution 污染

📞 *打電話問老師問題*

1. Do you believe pollution is a world-wide problem ?
   你相信污染是個全球性的問題嗎？

2. Do you think Taiwan is polluted ?
   你認爲台灣已受到污染了嗎？

3. What do you think is Taiwan's worst pollution problem ?
   你認爲台灣最嚴重的污染問題是什麼？

4. Do you believe it is wrong to litter ? 你認爲亂丟垃圾有錯嗎？

5. Do you try to reduce the amount of garbage you produce ?
   你是否盡量減少製造垃圾？

6. Do you try to recycle paper, plastic, metal and glass ?
   你是否回收紙張、塑膠、金屬和玻璃呢？

7. Do you think pollution is a threat to people's health ?
   你認爲污染威脅到人體的健康嗎？

8. Do you think pollution is a threat to wildlife ?
   你認爲污染對野生生態造成威脅嗎？

9. Do you think it is possible to solve Taiwan's pollution
   problems ? 你認爲台灣的污染問題可能解決嗎？

10. How do you think the government can decrease pollution ?
    你覺得政府可以如何減少污染？

11. How do you think factories can decrease pollution ?
    你覺得工廠可以如何減少污染？

📞 *打電話和老師討論問題*

Dialogue 1

老師：Do you believe pollution is a world-wide problem ?
你相信污染是個全球性的問題嗎？

學生：Yes. I've heard that most of the world's cities have pollution problems. The oceans and deserts are also polluted because of test-explosions of nuclear weapons.
是的，我聽說全世界大部分都市都有污染問題。海洋、沙漠也因為核武試爆而受到污染。

老師：Do you think Taiwan is polluted ?
你認為台灣已受到污染嗎？

學生：Absolutely. Taiwan has gotten much dirtier since I was a child. Wherever you go, there is always trash.
絕對有。從我小時候開始，台灣已變得愈形髒亂。無論走到那兒，總是會有垃圾。

老師：What do you think is Taiwan's worst pollution problem ?
你認為台灣最嚴重的污染問題是什麼？

學生：I think Taiwan's worst pollution problem is garbage. I wonder where we will put it all in the future.
我認為台灣最嚴重的污染問題是垃圾。我在想，將來我們能把它放到那裡。

**

explosion (ɪk'sploʒən) *n.* 爆炸
absolutely ('æbsə,lutlɪ ,,æbsə'lutlɪ) *adv.* 絕對地
garbage ('gɑrbɪdʒ) *n.* 垃圾

Dialogue 2

老師： Do you believe it is wrong to litter?
你認為亂丟垃圾有錯嗎？

學生： Yes, I think litter is disgusting. People should hold onto their litter until they find a garbage receptacle.
是的，我覺得垃圾很討人厭。在找到垃圾桶之前，大家應該把垃圾拿著。

老師： Do you try to reduce the amount of garbage you produce?
你是否盡量減少製造垃圾？

學生： Yes. I try to find new uses for containers, jars and bottles. I also try to write on both sides of paper.
是的，我試著尋找容器和瓶瓶罐罐的可用之處。我也嘗試在紙張的兩面都寫字。

老師： Do you try to recycle paper, plastic, metal and glass?
你是否嘗試回收紙張、塑膠、金屬和玻璃？

學生： Yes. I rinse out and save recyclable materials. Once a week, a recycling truck comes through my neighborhood to collect the materials.
是的，我清洗並貯藏可回收的物品。每個星期，回收車都會經過我家附近一次，收集資源。

**

litter (ˈlɪtɚ) v. 丟垃圾；n. 垃圾　　disgusting (dɪsˈgʌstɪŋ) adj. 令人厭惡的
receptacle (rɪˈsɛptəkḷ) n. 容器　　container (kənˈtenɚ) n. 容器
rinse (rɪns) v. 洗滌

Dialogue 3

老師：Do you think pollution is a threat to people's health？
你認為污染威脅到人體的健康嗎？

學生：Yes. If the air and water are dirty, people can get sick from the pollution. Dirty air often exasperates people who have asthma.
是的，如果空氣和水不乾淨，人們就會因污染而生病。骯髒的空氣也會使氣喘患者的病情加重。

老師：Do you think pollution is a threat to wildlife？
你認為污染對野生生態造成威脅嗎？

學生：Definitely. Pollution makes it very difficult for wild plants, animals and fish to survive. If we consume polluted animals, we might get sick or even poisoned.
絕對會。污染使野生植物、動物和魚類難以生存。如果我們攝食遭污染的動物，我們可能會得病甚至中毒。

老師：Do you think it is possible to solve Taiwan's pollution problems？ 你認為台灣的污染問題可能解決嗎？

學生：I hope so. I think both the people and the government will have to work hard to clean up Taiwan. The government should make more laws to control the pollution, and the factory owners should *behave themselves* --not *dump toxic materials at will*.
我希望可以。我認為民眾和政府都必須一同努力來淨化台灣。政府應該制定更多法律來管制污染，而工廠業者也應該自我約束——不要隨意傾到有毒物質。

**
exasperate〔ɪgˈzæspəˌret, ɛg-〕v. 增劇　　asthma〔ˈæsmə, ˈæzmə〕n. 氣喘
survive〔səˈvaɪv〕v. 生存　　consume〔kənˈsum, -ˈsjum〕v. 攝食
behave oneself 守規矩　　dump〔dʌmp〕v. 傾倒
toxic〔ˈtɑksɪk〕adj. 有毒的　　*at will* 隨意

40. *Environmentalism*
環保主義

📞 *打電話問老師問題*

1. Do you care about Taiwan's environment ?
   你關心台灣的環境嗎？

2. Do you recycle used newspapers ?
   你有做舊報紙的資源回收嗎？

3. What can you do to improve Taiwan's environment ?
   你可以如何來改善台灣的環境？

4. Do you recycle PET bottles ?
   你有做保特瓶回收嗎？

5. What can you do to improve your own environment ?
   你可以如何來改善你的環境呢？

6. Are you an environmentalist ?
   你是環境保護主義者嗎？

7. Do you conserve water and electricity?
   你節約用水和用電嗎？

8. How long do you think it will be before the people of Taiwan get serious about recycling ?
   你認為要多久，台灣人民才會用心做資源回收？

9. Do you think it is possible to recycle more than 80% of everyday trash and garbage ?
   你認為要回收百分之八十以上每天的廢物和垃圾，有可能嗎？

📞 *打電話和老師討論問題*

Dialogue 1

老師： Do you care about Taiwan's environment?
你關心台灣的環境嗎？

學生： Of course I do. I consider it my duty as a resident in Taiwan to care for the environment. However, most people just don't care.
當然關心。我認為去關心自己的環境是我身為台灣居民的本分。然而，大多數人就是不在乎。

老師： Do you recycle used newspapers?
你有做舊報紙的回收嗎？

學生： I do it whenever I can. But it is hard for one to re-cycle paper in Taiwan as there aren't many recycling bins around, and it is a very big hassle to get paper recycled.
我盡我所能的去做，但是在台灣紙張的回收不易，因為周遭沒有很多回收桶，而且要把紙張作回收處理有很大的困難。

老師： What can we do to improve Taiwan's environment?
我們可以如何來改善台灣的環境？

學生： The government needs to *get its act together*, and pro-mote recycling on a larger and more realistic scale, not just *all talk and no action*. For a start, we need more recycling bins.
政府需要展開行動，並大規模實際地提倡資源回收，而不是空談沒有行動。首先，我們需要更多的回收桶。

** ————————————

resident (ˈrɛzədənt) *n.* 居住者　　recycle (rɪˈsaɪkḷ) *v.* 再生利用
bin (bɪn) *n.* 貯藏箱　　hassle (ˈhæsḷ) *n.* 奮戰　　promote (prəˈmot) *v.* 提倡

Dialogue 2

老師： Do you recycle PET bottles？

你有做寶特瓶回收嗎？

學生： Yes. I take them to my local shop, and for every empty bottle I get a little money back, too. But I do it for the environment rather than the money.

有。我把空瓶拿到我們當地的商店，每個空瓶可以換回一些錢。不過我這麼做是為了環境而不是錢。

老師： What can we do to improve our own environment？

我們可以如何來改善自己的環境？

學生： How about wasting less resources to start with, rather than worrying about what you're going to do with the empty bottles and cans afterwards？ *We waste more resources than we think*.

何不以浪費較少的資源開始著手，而不要事後才擔心該如何處理空瓶罐？我們所浪費的資源超過我們所能想像的。

老師： Are you an environmentalist？

你是環境保護主義者嗎？

學生： I don't consider myself an environmentalist. I certainly don't go around protesting about the environment and *go on hunger strikes*, but *I do what is within my powers* to protect and conserve the environment.

我不認為自己是環境保護主義者。我絕不會四處為環境抗議或絕食，但我會在自己能力所及之下，去愛護和保存我們的環境。

**

resource (rɪˋsors , ˋrisors) *n.* 資源

start with 開始　　protest (prəˋtɛst) *v.* 抗議

strike (straɪk) *n.* 罷工　　conserve (kənˋsɝv) *v.* 保護；保存

Dialogue 3

老師：Do you conserve water and electricity？
你節約用水和用電嗎？

學生：I try to. For example, when I cook I don't keep the water running, and I turn off the lights when I am not using them rather than leaving them on.
我嘗試在做。比方說，做飯時，我不讓水一直流，不用燈時，我會關掉，而不讓它們亮著。

I also have a brick in the cistern at home which saves water every time I flush my toilet.
我也在我們家馬桶的水箱裡放了一塊磚，每次沖水時都可省一些水。

老師：How long do you think it will be before the people of Taiwan get serious about recycling？
你認為要多久，台灣人民才會用心做資源回收？

學生：When it becomes apparent that the environment is being destroyed！Unfortunately signs of this are showing already.
當環境被破壞得很明顯的時候吧！很不幸地，這個徵兆已經出現。

People are too concerned with other things such as making money to worry about the environment.
人們太在乎賺錢等其他事情，而忽略了對環境的關心。

** ─────────────────

brick〔brɪk〕*n.* 磚　　cistern〔'sɪstən〕*n.* 水箱
flush〔flʌʃ〕*v.* 沖水　　figure〔'fɪgɚ , 'fɪgjɚ〕*n.* 數字

老師：Do you think it is possible to recycle more than 80 % of everyday trash and garbage ?

你認為，要回收百分之八十以上每天的廢物和垃圾，有可能嗎？

學生：We shouldn't care about how much we can recycle, but how much we try to recycle. Once we've done our best then no one can complain. And I believe that if we all try hard, 80 % is a realistic figure.

我們不要去管能回收多少，只問自己盡了多少力去做。一旦我們盡全力，沒有人會抱怨。而且我相信，如果我們都努力去試，百分之八十是個可達到的數據。

☆ 環保相關語彙

battery〔'bætərɪ〕*n.* 電池　　　mercury〔'mɜkjərɪ〕*n.* 水銀

recharge〔ri'tʃɑrdʒ〕*v.* 再充電　toxic〔'tɑksɪk〕*adj.* 有毒的

disposable〔dɪ'spozəbḷ〕*adj.* 用完即丟的

landfill〔'lænd,fɪl〕*n.* 掩埋場

incinerator〔ɪn'sɪnə,retɚ〕*n.* 焚化爐

plastic〔'plæstɪk〕*adj.* 塑膠的

deforestation〔dɪ,fɔrɪs'teʃən〕*n.* 砍伐森林

ozone〔'ozon〕*n.* 臭氧　　　ozone layer 臭氧層

fuel〔'fjuəl〕*n.* 燃料　　　pesticide〔'pɛstɪsaɪd〕*n.* 殺蟲劑

detergent〔dɪ'tɜdʒənt〕*n.* 清潔劑

refuse〔'rɛfjus〕*n.* 垃圾；拋棄物

carcinogeon〔kɑr'sɪnədʒən〕*n.* 致癌物

degradable〔dɪ'gredəbḷ〕*adj.* 可腐蝕的

Environmental Protection Administration 環保署

拿起電話，馬上就可以說英語！

結合電腦與通訊科技，欣語社為您設計「**克拉瑪空中外語交談園地**」，以最方便、經濟、效率的休閒式方法，使您學習外語會話成為舉手之勞。

1. 以會員制**購卡**方式，一卡可通美、日語。經您授權，別人亦可使用。

2. 在系統的時間內（全年無休），只要有電話機，可隨時地和老外練習外語，而不耽誤您正常作息。

3. 會員卡無使用期限，且每次談話**時間亦無限制**。

4. 電腦自動計時，並告知您剩餘時間。

5. 您的花費只有傳統一對一費用的一半或更少，同時省去餐費、交通費及時間。

6. 每次對談之前您可設定喜歡的話題，及預備些字彙或造句，我們的外籍會員依據您所表達之外語程度，以適當之談話速度，及深淺字句和您雙向溝通，讓您在閒談式的心情下，增進外語能力和信心。

7. 假設您正從事國際商務，只需一通電話，便有外籍秘書或活字典在電話彼端，即刻為您解決外文上的疑難。

8. 您每次談話對象，可能都是不同之外籍會員，除可加強適應不同之腔調外，亦可增加不同生活體驗及擴展國際視野。

★ **入會費及通話費如下：**

入會費	美語卡（日本語卡）		通話費
500 元	每次購	10 小時	2,800 元
		20 小時	5,200 元
		40 小時	10,000 元
免費	續 卡 之 會 員（本 人）		

☞凡購買 *You Can Call Me* 一書的讀者，可利用書後所附之劃撥單、訂購單，享受**免入會費**的優待。

★ **通話時間**

美語卡：早上 9 點至晚上 12 點　　日本語卡：晚上 7 點至晚上 11 點。

☞ 通話專線 *12* 線，不用擔心佔線。

★ **購卡方式：**

1. 利用附表之劃撥單（帳號 18291332，戶名：欣語社）、**信用卡訂購單**，填妥即可。
2. 來社購卡，週一至週六 AM10:00 ～ PM10:00
3. 送卡收款：暫限台北市內，但須配合本社時間。

The Foreign Members（Teachers）Reference
外籍會員背景參考表

NAME	DEGREE	EDUCATION	NATIONALITY
Mr. Chris Smith	Bachelor	Yale, Maryland	USA
Mr. Tom	Bachelor	James Madison	USA
Mr. George	Bachelor	Rutgers University	USA
Mr. Steve	Bachelor	UCLA	USA
Mr. Mark	Bachelor	UCLA	USA
Mr. John	Bachelor	Hawaii University	USA
Ms. Diana	Master	U.C. Berkeley	USA
Mr. Gregor	Bachelor	U.C. Santa Cruz	USA
Ms. Marie	Master	Irvine MBA	A.B.C
Mr. Romeo	Bachelor	Mapua Institution	OS Chinese
Ms. Brenda	Bachelor	Philippine University	Filipino
Ms. Jeanette	Bachelor	Delasaile University	OS Chinese
Ms. Emily	Bachelor	Delasaile University	OS Chinese

凡參加「克拉瑪空中外語交談園地」之會員，除免費提供 TOPICS 資料，讓您加強聽講會話能力，我們亦增加下列服務項目：

★ **英文書信、商業文件、寫作等之修改與修辭** ☎ *02-7516278*

已加入（克拉瑪空中外語交談園地）之會員才有附帶服務，讓您除

加強外語會話能力外,亦可提升層次,說寫俱佳。其計費方式將依文件難易,從會員卡使用時數中扣除,請將您需要修改之文章,傳眞或郵寄給欣語社。

★ **在校學生英文課業電話輔導** ☎ *02-7516278*

在系統通話時間,都可依據各級英文(國中、高中、大專院校)內容,爲您做文法解析、發音糾正、內容及寫作之討論,加強您聽講能力之課業電話輔導。讓您輕輕鬆鬆應付英文課業,而不再是面對壓力,進而培養學習英文的興趣。

★ **Cassette Telephone Recorder**
　(卡式電話錄放音機;可自行錄製英,日語教學錄音帶)

適用於桌上型或手提式有線電話,在您跟外籍老師練習會話時,即可利用一般錄音帶做線上雙面錄音;除事後可重複聽帶以加強聽力外,亦可檢討自己發音、文法正確與否?對話內容是否適切?換言之,您可在家裡錄製自己所需之英、日語教學錄音帶,此機除使用於電話外,亦可用作一般之錄音機,如有需要請來電洽詢。

★ **英語會談諮詢,每次 200 元**

每週五下午 7:30 至 9:00,本社現場備有外語助理,可協助會員英語任何方面之請益(因場地有限,只接受空中外語交談園地之會員參與)。您可視需要隨時駕臨,每次酌收費用 NT$200 元。

欣語社
克拉瑪語音廣場
台北市忠孝東路四段 155 號 11 樓之 3
TEL:(02)751-6278
FAX:(02)751-0017
AM10:00 ～ PM10:00

收據號碼：

郵政劃撥儲金存款收據單

收款人	帳號	1	8	2	9	1	3	3	2	中心局郵戳
	戶名	欣 語 社								

新臺幣
（請用壹、貳、參、肆、伍、陸、柒、捌、玖、零等大寫並於數末加一整字）

寄款人　姓名　住址（郵遞區號）　電話

經辦局郵戳

主管：

經辦員：

證連用線請內勿填機寫器蓋印。

主管：

經辦員：

郵政劃撥儲金存款通知單

帳號未滿入位數者，帳號前空格請填 0。

收款人	帳號	1	8	2	9	1	3	3	2
	帳戶	欣 語 社							

新臺幣
（請用壹、貳、參、肆、伍、陸、柒、捌、玖、零等大寫並於數末加一整字）

寄款人　姓名　住址（郵遞區號）　電話

經辦局郵戳

本聯經登帳後隨郵政劃撥儲金收支詳情單寄交帳戶。

○◎存款
本收據由郵
局以機器列
印，如非機
器列印或經
塗改，或無
收款郵局收
訖章者無
效。此聯由
郵局蓋用收
據章後交寄
款人收執為
憑，惟本單
不作收據
用。

請 存 款 人 注 意

一、帳號、戶名及寄款人姓名、住址請詳細填寫，以免誤寄。抵付票據之存款，務請於交換前一天存入。

二、每筆存款至少須在新台幣十元以上。

三、倘金額塗改時請另換存款填寫。

四、本存款單不得黏貼或附寄任何文件。

五、本存款金額業經電腦登帳後或本存款單已經受理郵局寄出者，不得申請撤回。

欄

□ 美語卡 □ 10 小時 NT$ 2,800 元
□ 20 小時 NT$ 5,200 元
□ 40 小時 NT$ 10,000 元

註：本寄款人為 You Can Call Me 之讀者，得享有免付入會費 NT$ 500 元之優待。

此欄係備寄款人與帳戶通訊之用，惟所作附言應於關於該次劃撥事項為限。**否則應請換單另填。**

欣 語 社 01-016-0740-3

美語卡訂購郵寄（傳眞）信用卡付款辦法：

1. 郵寄訂購：請塡妥本單寄台北市忠孝東路 4 段 155 號 11 樓之 3

2. 傳眞訂購：請塡妥本單傳眞 02-751-0017 卽可

付款方式：□ VISA CARD　　□ MASTER CARD
　　　　　□ 聯合信用卡　　□ JCB CARD

持卡人姓名：_____

信用卡號：_____　有效期限：____ 年 ____ 月止

持卡人身份證字號：_____

持卡人地址：_____

訂購日期：_____ 年 _____ 月 _____ 日

電話：(H) _____　(O) _____

持卡人簽名：_____　（與信用卡簽名相同）

會話時數：□ 十小時　　□ 二十小時　　□ 四十小時

金額：NT$ _____　授權碼：_____　（空白由本社塡寫）

註：本持卡人爲 You Can Call Me 之讀者，得享有免付入會費 NT$500
　　元之優待。

寄會員卡地址：_____

持卡人同意依照信用卡使用約定，經使用或訂購物品，均應按所示之全
部金額，付款予發卡銀行。

特別推薦：最實用、好學的會話教材

●5分鐘學會說英文①②③冊●

張 齡 編譯

「五分鐘學會說英文」是根據美國中央情報局的特殊記憶訓練法，所精心編輯而成的。您只要花五分鐘，就能記住一種實況，且在短時間內融會貫通，靈活運用。

本書最符合現代人的需要，用字淺顯，內容都是日常生活必備的，句子簡短，易懂、易記。例如想請外國朋友吃中飯，該怎麼說呢？本書教您最實用最普遍的講法：*Lunch is on me.*

「五分鐘學會說英文」每冊均分為八十課。每課由一句話揭示主題，再以三個不同的會話實況，使您徹底了解使用的場合。三個會話實況以後，列有「舉一反三」，包含五組對話，幫助您推展主題的運用範圍。凡是重要的單字、片語，均詳列於每課之後；對於特殊的注意事項和使用方法，則另附有背景說明。

錄音帶採用兩遍英文的跟讀練習，隨時可聽可學。

◎書每冊150元，每冊書另有錄音帶四卷500元。

● SITUATION 39 ●
Lunch is on me.

Dialogue 2

A : Miss, may I have the check ?
　小姐，請把帳單給我好嗎？

B : How much do I owe you, Jane ?
　珍，我要付你多少？

A : Nothing. *Lunch is on me.*
　不必了。中飯我請客。

B : Thank you. Next time lunch is on me. 謝謝你。下回中飯我請。

A : O.K. That's a deal.
　好的。一言為定。

B : Let's go. 我們走吧。

〔舉一反三〕

A : This *lunch is on me*. 中飯我請客。

B : Thank you. 謝謝你。

A : Are you buying dinner tonight ?
　今晚晚餐你付帳嗎？

B : Yes. *Dinner is on me.*
　是的，晚餐我請客。

A : Let's go Dutch. 我們分攤吧。

B : No, *it's my treat*. 不，我請客。

A : *Drinks are on me*. 酒由我請客。

B : What's the occasion? 要慶祝什麼？

特別推薦

全國最完整的文法書 ☆☆☆

文法寶典

▶ 劉 毅 編著

這是一套想學好英文的人必備的工具書,作者積多年豐富的教學經驗,針對大家所不了解和最容易犯錯的地方,編寫成一套完整的文法書。

本書編排方式與眾不同,首先給讀者整體的概念,再詳述文法中的細節部分,內容十分完整。文法說明以圖表爲中心,一目了然,並且務求深入淺出。無論您在考試中或其他書中所遇到的任何不了解的問題,或是您感到最煩惱的文法問題,查閱**文法寶典**均可迎刃而解。例如:哪些副詞可修飾名詞或代名詞?(P.228);什麼是介副詞?(P.543);那些名詞可以當副詞用?(P.100);倒裝句(P.629)、省略句(P.644)等特殊構句,爲什麼倒裝?爲什麼省略?原來的句子是什麼樣子?在**文法寶典**裏都有詳盡的說明。

例如,有人學了**觀念錯誤的**「假設法現在式」的公式,

If + 現在式動詞……,主詞 + shall(will, may, can)+ 原形動詞

只會造:If it rains, I will stay at home.

而不敢造:If you *are* right, I *am* wrong.

      If I *said* that, I *was* mistaken.

      (If 子句不一定用在假設法,也可表示條件子句的直說法。)

可見如果學文法不求徹底了解,反而成爲學習英文的絆腳石,對於這些易出錯的地方,我們都特別加以說明(詳見 P.356)。

文法寶典每冊均附有練習,只要讀完本書、做完練習,您必定信心十足,大幅提高對英文的興趣與實力。

◉ 全套五冊,售價 **900** 元。市面不售,請直接向本公司購買。

革命性英語學習新方法

說英文高手①

特別推薦

➤ 劉 毅 編著

劉 毅老師繼「一天背好 1000 個英單字」後，又有一個革命性的新發明。「說英文高手①」出版後，即造成轟動。

☆ 三句爲一組，一次說三句 ☆

人類的短暫記憶有限，如這個數字「411213311」很難背，但是分開來，「411－213－311」就較容易背。如再排成「211－311－411」就不可能忘記。英文一句一句背，容易忘記，但是一次背三句相關連的句子，就不容易忘。

☆ 容易記，不容易忘 ☆

「說英文高手」的句子，都是摘錄自美國人常用的會話，而且隨時可用得到，可以和外國人說，可以和中國人說，也可以自言自語說。例如：你隨時可說："What a beauitful day it is !"（多麼美好的一天！）再接著說：It's not too hot. It's not too cold. It's just right. 像這樣的句子，就是容易記、不容易忘，隨時可以用得到。

☆ 跟著錄音帶說，效果特佳 ☆

「說英文高手」錄音帶的製作，以三句爲一組，第一次先用慢速，你可跟著外國老師唸。第二次用正常速度，一次唸三句。最後一次用正常速度唸完整個單元。只要利用上下班的時間，或等公車的時間，聽聽錄音帶，跟著唸，很快地你就可以一次說三句以上，成爲說英文高手。你的朋友見到你會說：

Your English is improving.
Your English is progressing.
Your English is getting better.

◉ 書180元／錄音帶四卷500元

全省各大書局均售

•心得筆記欄•

•心得筆記欄•

Editorial Staff

- 編著 / 吳 濱 伶

- 校訂 / 劉　毅・陳瑠琍・謝靜芳・蔡琇瑩・莊心怡

- 校閱 / Wen-tao Chan ・ Nicole Woo ・ Thomas Deneau
  Gregor Downey ・ Fred Mansfield

- 封面設計 / 陳怡靜

- 版面設計 / 張鳳儀

- 版面構成 / 陳怡靜・吳濱伶

- 打字 / 吳秋香・黃淑貞

All rights reserved. No part of this publication
may be reproduced without the prior permission
of Learning Publishing Company.
本書版權爲學習出版公司所有，翻印必究。

國立中央圖書館出版品預行編目資料

```
You Can Call Me / 吳濱伶編著        --初版--
  〔臺北市〕：學習發行；
  〔臺北縣新店市〕：學英總經銷，1996〔民85〕
     面；公分
  ISBN 957-519-464-0（平裝）


  1. 英國語言—會話
805.188                                  85000262
```

You Can Call Me

編　　　著 / 吳　濱　伶
發　行　所 / 學習出版有限公司　　　☎ (02) 7045525
郵　撥帳號 / 0512727-2 學習出版社帳戶
登　記　證 / 局版台業 2179 號
印　刷　所 / 裕強彩色印刷有限公司 n
台 北 門 市 / 台北市許昌街 10 號 2 F　　☎ (02) 3314060・3319209
台 中 門 市 / 台中市綠川東街 32 號 8 F 23 室　　☎ (04) 2232838
台灣總經銷 / 學英文化事業公司　　　☎ (02) 2187307
美國總經銷 / Evergreen Book Store　　☎ (818) 2813622

售價：新台幣一百八十元正
1997 年 11 月 1 日一版二刷

ISBN 957-519-464-0　　　　　　　　版權所有・翻印必究